KERIS AND OTHER MALAY WEAPONS

Keris and other Malay Weapons

G. B. GARDNER
Johore Civil Service

Edited by
B. LUMSDEN MILNE

ORCHID PRESS

G. B. Gardner (1884-1964)
KERIS AND OTHER MALAY WEAPONS

First published 1936 in an edition limited to 150 copies.
Reprinted 2009.

ORCHID PRESS
P.O. Box 1046
Silom Post Office,
Bangkok 10504, Thailand

© Orchid Press 2009
Protected by copyright under the terms of the International Copyright Union: all rights reserved. Except for fair use in book reviews, no part of this publication may be reproduced in any form or by any means, electronic or mechanical, including photocopying, recording, or by any information storage or retrieval system without prior permission in writing from the copyright holder.

Cover image : Hilt of an ancient *kĕris* from the now vanished Malay kingdom of Champa; private collection, Singapore.

ISBN-10: 974-8304-29-9
ISBN-13: 978-974-8304-29-8

AUTHOR'S FOREWORD

I venture to hope that this little book may be of interest and assistance to collectors of weapons. It is possible also that ethnologists may be interested in the customs and superstitions connected with these weapons and their origin.

The photographs are almost entirely of weapons in my own collection. I shall be very pleased to show this collection to anyone interested, who cares to write to me, care of my publishers or of The Crown Agents for the Colonies.

I should like to express my indebtedness to:

The Hon. Y. M. Ĕngku Abdul Aziz b. Abdul Majid, Hon. C.M.G., Dato Mĕntĕri Besar, Johore, and The Hon. Y. M. Ĕngku Abdul Hamid b. Abdul Majid, for their kindness in showing me their valuable old weapons.

Pawang Salleh for much helpful information on superstitions,

Dr. A. N. J. Th. a' Th. van der Hoop, Secretary of the Batavia Society and Dr. Poerbatjaraka for their assistance during my visits to the Batavia Museum,

The late Mr. Cyril Blair Cooper for presenting me with some of his MSS,

Professor van Stein Callenfels for information as to the age of *k. majapahit* and for an anecdote of Javanese warfare,

Mrs. A. Savage Bailey, Librarian of Raffles Library, Singapore, for access to and assistance with works of reference,

Mr. F. N. Chasen and Mr. H. D. Collings for placing the resources of Raffles Museum at my disposal,

and to

Sir Richard O. Winstedt, C.M.G., D.Litt., K.B.E., for his friendly interest, advice and help extending over many years.

G. B. Gardner
January 1936

CONTENTS

1. *Kĕris*.
    - I. General 1
    - II. Origin 4
    - III. Blade 7
    - IV. Hilt 12
    - V. Sheath 18
    - VI. Classification 23
    - VII. Various 38
    - VIII. Legends And Superstitions 42
    - IX. The *Kĕris* Today 51
2. Daggers 53
3. Swords 56
4. Spears 72
5. Cannon 78
6. Small Arms 85
7. Bows and Arrows. Blowpipes 88
8. Miscellaneous Weapons. I. Old 91
    - Miscellaneous Weapons. II. Modern 99
9. Dayak Weapons 101

10. Appendices
    A. Malay Warfare 104
    B. Malay War Dress and Armour 107
    C. Malay Fortifications 111
    D. Invulnerability 114
11. Glossary 119
12. Bibliography 131
13. About the Author 132

Publisher's Notes:

Comments and notes added by B. Lumsden Milne, the editor of the first edition of this volume, will be followed with the attribution (BLM). Additional notes contributed by the editor of the present, Orchid Press, edition may be identified by the attribution (Ed.)

The photographic images in the first edition of this book were of uneven quality, and their original reproduction was not optimal. The objects illustrated were almost all drawn from the extensive collection of the author; however, this collection has long since been broken up and widely dispersed, so it has not been possible to track down the objects for rephotography. It is felt that the illustrations, even as they are, record an important collection of artefacts and it is hoped that allowance will be made for their quality.

Parts of a *Kĕris* and Sheath

(Nos. refer to the drawings on the opposite page).

Fig. 1:
1. *Tangkai* or *paksi*: tang.
2. *Ganja*: guard.
3. *Gandik*.
4. *Lambai gajah*: elephant's tusk.
5. *Bĕlalai gajah*: elephant's trunk.
6. *Kambing kachang*.
7. *Janggut*.
8. *Tulang kĕris*: raised centre rib (rare).
9. *Hujong kĕris*: the point (some times called *mata*, though this properly refers to the whole blade).
10. *Aring*: the pointed side of the *ganja*.
11. *Dagu*: the blunt side of the *ganja*.

Note: Nos. 4 & 5 are nearly always on the same side of the blade as No. 11.

Fig. 2:
1. *Hulu kĕris*: the hilt.
2. *Pĕndongkok*: cup at base of hilt.
3. *Sampir*: crosspiece of sheath
4. *Sarong*: (the part covering the blade is strictly the *sarong*, but the term is applied to the whole sheath).
5. *Buntut*: chap on tip of sheath.

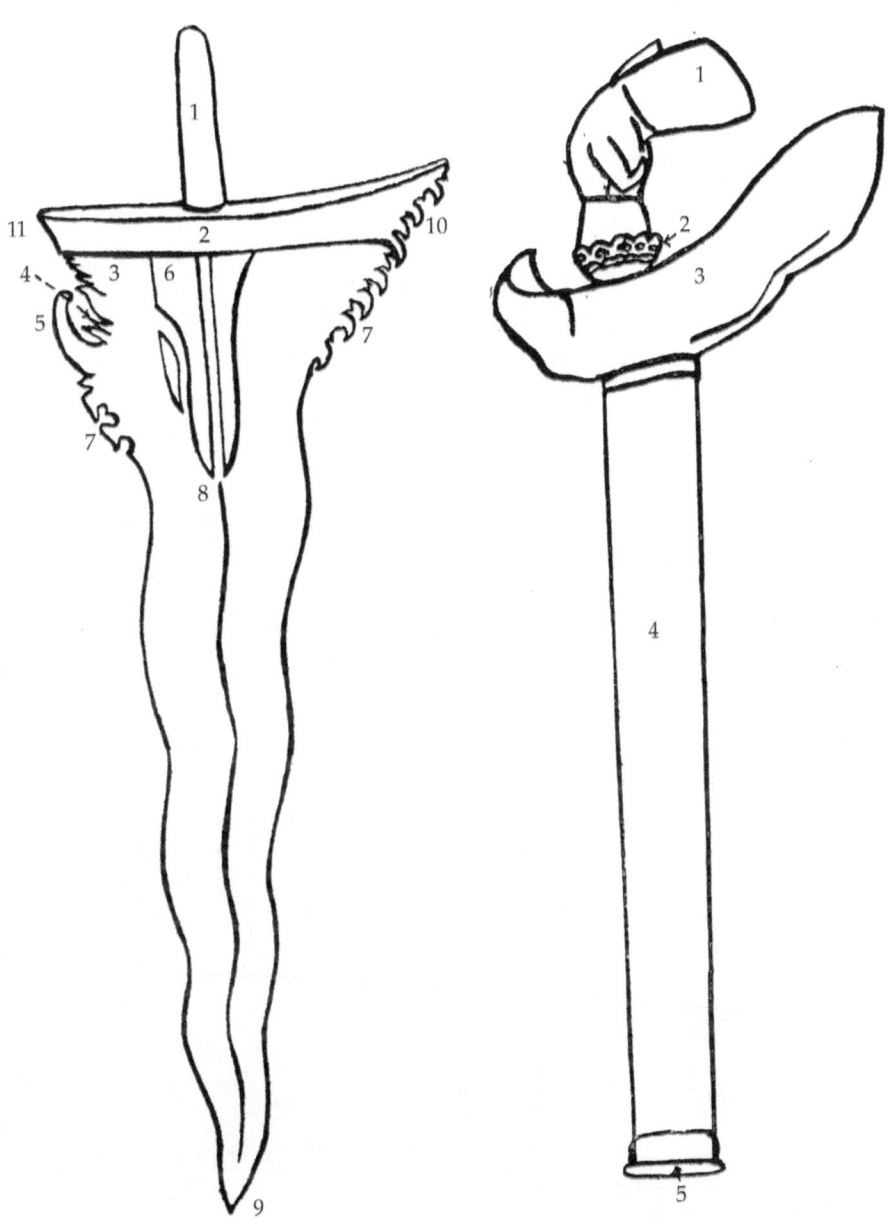

1. & 2. Parts of a *Kĕris* and Sheath.

CHAPTER 1

THE KĚRIS

I. GENERAL.

The *kěris* is undoubtedly the distinctive Malay weapon. It is necessary however, to define a *kěris*. It is primarily a dagger with a handle set at an angle to the blade, a sort of pistol grip in fact, to enable the wielder to thrust.

The *kěris* is I believe unique, in being the dagger with the greatest reach, compared with the total length of the weapon. All other daggers are held in one of two ways (see Plate 3 Nos. 1 & 2) but the *kěris* is held as in Plate 3 No. 3 and with it there is a greater reach, although the thrust lacks some of the force derived from the swing of the weapon held as in (1) or (2).

Argensola, writing in 1609 says: "At Menancabo[1] excellent weapons called creeses[2] best weapons in all the Orient."

The *kěris* is a rapier in fact. The European rapier is long and needs a long handle to balance it. The *kěris* being short, a short handle is enough for its original form; but as men fought, the *kěris* became longer and heavier. Two more forms were evolved. First, the Sumatran rapier *kěris, k. bahari;* this being long, the handle had to be straightened out to balance it, and it acquired almost the European rapier form; and secondly, the *sundang,* the Malay broadsword.

The edge of the blade near the hilt, also the *ganja,* are usually dentiform. Part of this ornamental work is called *janggut* and is so made in order to catch an opposing blade. Nearer the hilt this work is called *Bĕlalai gajah* and *lambai gajah.* In very old *kěris* this clearly represents an elephant's trunk and tusk, but is now rather conventionalised. A

[1] Měnangkabau.
[2] Kěris.

KERIS AND OTHER MALAY WEAPONS

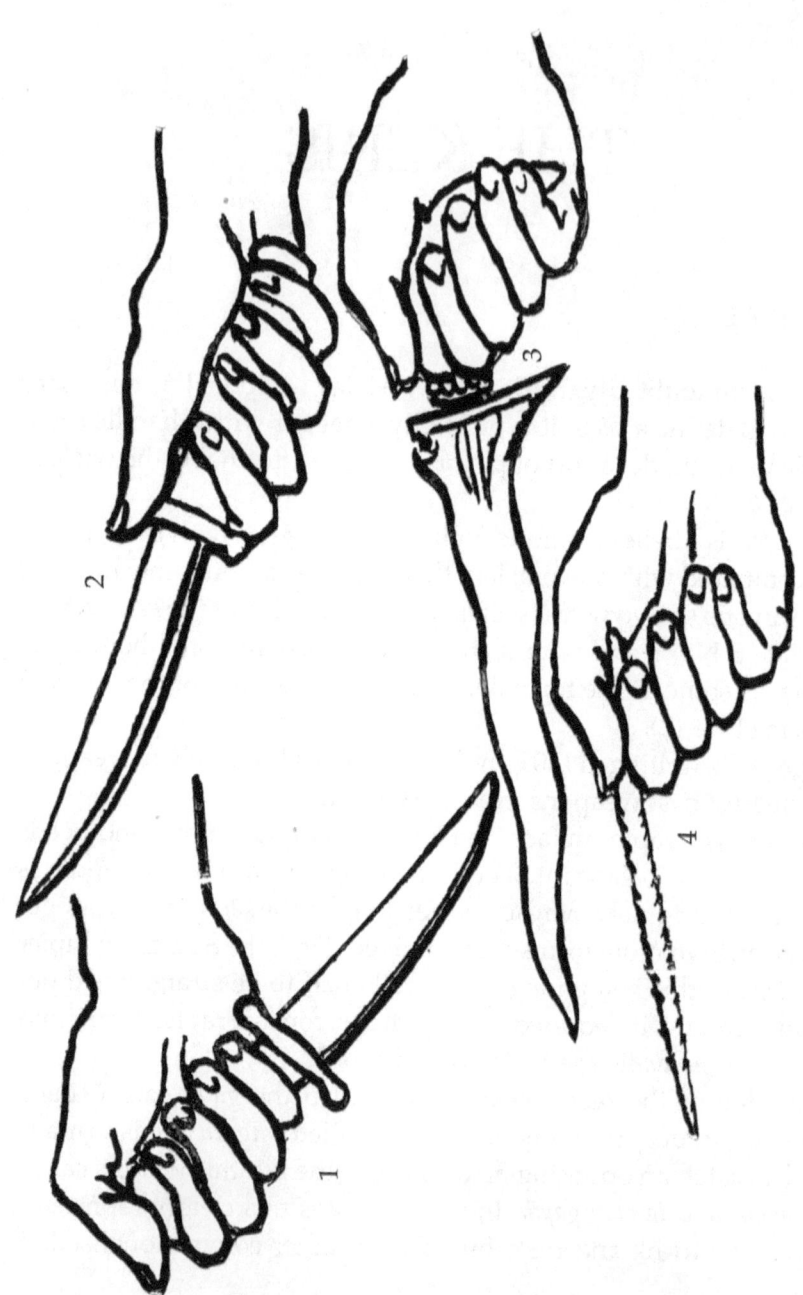

3. Dagger grips and *kĕris* grip.

CHAPTER 1: KĔRIS

stone carved in the form of an elephant's trunk was a favourite motif in Hindu Java. One such stone now in Raffles Museum, has been found on the Johore River, also small ornaments of similar shape in earthenware. Another is in Malacca.

This motif was presumably the sign of the elephant god, a symbol of strength and power, and so was considered a lucky thing to have on a *kĕris*, even after its origin was forgotten. It is nearly always found on the blunt side of the *ganja* though occasionally on the sharp side, and *kĕris* are known that have one on each side.

The old European authors speak of the *kĕris* as a poisoned weapon. In modern times the *kĕris* is certainly not poisoned, although many types of *kĕris*, which were made small to economise iron, were poisoned: but as the *kĕris* got bigger it was found that it was deadly enough in itself.

The drawback to the use of poison is that it has to be continually renewed. Malay vegetable poisons are all wild and difficult to obtain. When the Malays were a village people and their weapons were small, poison was necessary and they obtained it. When the towns were formed, they could not get enough of the poison and found that with bigger and more efficient weapons they did not need it: but the poisons were still available and were used occasionally. D'Albuquerque[1] tells us that when attacking Malacca he lost many men from poisoned arrows and I think there is a basis for both European and Malay stories of poisoned *kĕris*.

It is known that poison was used in Europe in early times. The microlith arrowheads were useless without it, and hellebore has been used down the ages for this purpose, and the method cherished as a secret in some families. Payne Galloway[2] tells of the Spanish crossbow bolts, poisoned with hellebore, that, shot into a deer's leg, killed it before it had run two hundred yards. But in Europe, as, I believe, in Malaya,

---

[1] Afonso d'Albuquerque (1453-1515), a Portuguese nobleman and warrior, conquered the port of Malacca and claimed it as a colony of Portugal, after a bitter struggle, in 1511. (Ed.)

[2] Gardner's mention of 'Payne Galloway' (*sic*) is a reference to Sir Ralph Payne-Gallwey (1848-1916), the author of several books on weaponry as used in warfare and sport. Payne-Gallwey first published *The Crossbow* in 1903 (see Bibliography), the seminal work on this weapon and a volume that remains in print to the present day. (Ed.)

the weapon grew in efficiency until poison became unnecessary and the method of poisoning became the secret of the witch, or *pawang*.

II. ORIGIN.

What is the origin of a *kĕris*? Many people say it came from India, giving as reasons:

> (1) The *kĕris* is wavy and wavy weapons were used in India.
> (2) The Malays received their early civilisation from India, so the *kĕris* must have come from there.

I think the *kĕris* originated in Malaysia. The primitive Malay had no flint, but made various polished and unpolished instruments. These took time and labour and were not good weapons whatever they may have been as tools, but for the Malay fisherman there was a very effective natural weapon for which anyone who has trodden on the sting of an *ikan pari* (sting ray) will vouch.

Dr. Bianca saw a young man faint from the merest prick of a ray sting he was examining, (vide Gimlette: *Malay Poisons and Charm Cures*) and it must have occurred to some primitive man, that this would be a fine thing to stick into an enemy. The ray sting is barbed down the sides and anyone who held it like a knife and stabbed would poison his own hand and reduce the length of his reach and he would probably break the sting; but if held between the thumb and finger, with the butt against the base of the thumb it could be used with safety and this is the way to hold a small *kĕris majapahit*. A refinement would be the tying on of a bit of bark cloth. (See Plate 29 No. 2).

I made an experiment and found that when the cloth handle is grasped like a *kĕris* it resembles the *k. majapahit* hilt. The wielder of such a weapon would not be trying to reach the heart or other vital spot, he would jab and withdraw. His enemy would be paralysed with pain and could easily be finished off.

In excavations in the Dutch Indies, of the relics of Stone Age people, many *ikan pari* stings have been found, sometimes five or six days' journey from the sea, which shows that these people had some good use for them. I have no doubt they were used with bark cloth handles as *kĕris*.

When the poison became stale it could be repoisoned from a freshly caught ray or from Sakai arrow poisons. The bearer would only have to fight another man naked like himself.

The Malays would first know of metal weapons through trade, and these would be in the form the traders used (whoever they were) but the Malays having learned to work metal might well make blades in the form of the weapons they were used to, and a man used to a sting ray *kĕris* would use a small *k. majapahit* in the same way: a quick jab and withdraw. This, I think, explains the Malay belief that the *k. majapahit* is so venomous.

Most authorities say that the early *kĕris* was straight and that it only became wavy about the 15th century.

Personally I think the waves (*lok*) came from Indian weapons. The name of *sĕmpana kĕling* for a three waved *kĕris* suggests this. A primitive Indian weapon that is still used is made from ibex horn, round or split. Steel daggers are also made, imitating the waves of this horn and the Malays may have seen and copied them (see Plate 4). A nicely waved *kĕris* is very beautiful and it has a practical advantage in that it makes a much wider wound and will also work its way in and out among bones where a wider blade would stick. However, all Malays did not take kindly to the wavy *kĕris*. Many of the older men still say that the straight blade is the best, and certainly more blades seem to be made straight than wavy; that is, among blades that are made for use. The globe-trotter always wants a wavy blade and they are made for him.

KERIS AND OTHER MALAY WEAPONS

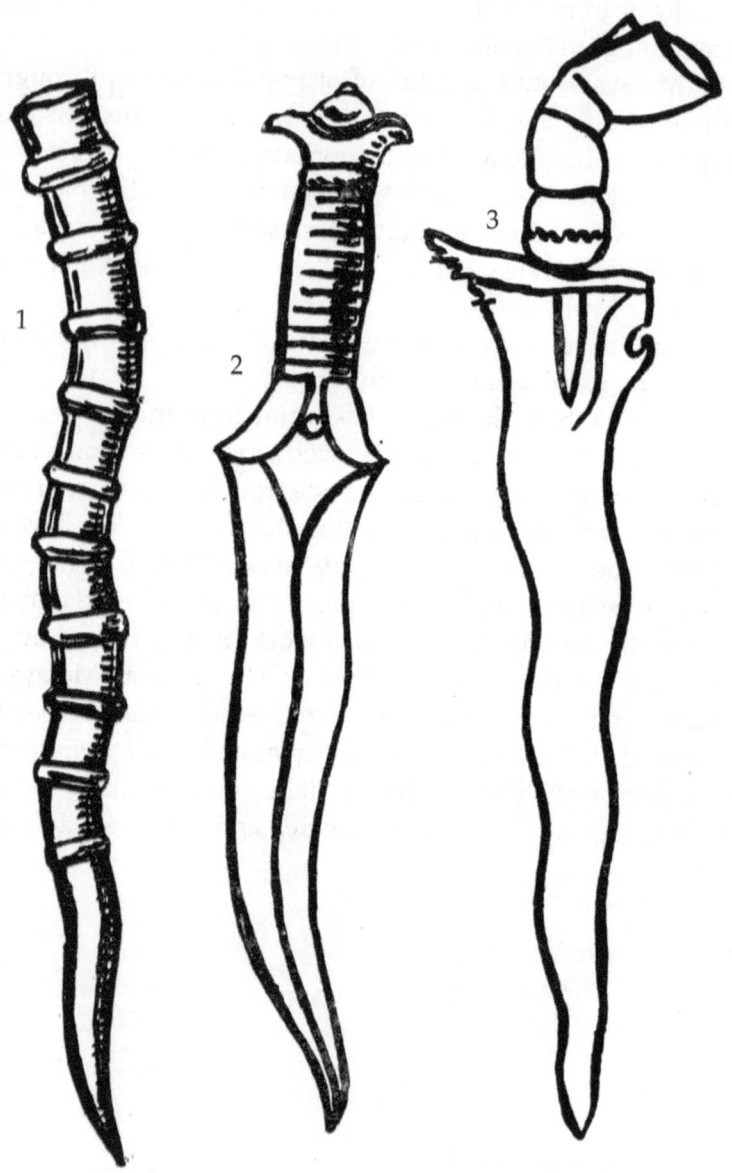

4. 1. Ibex horn. 2. Sinuous dagger. 3. *Kĕris*.

CHAPTER 1: KĔRIS

III. THE BLADE.

The first iron workers and *kĕris* makers in Malaya were called *pandai bĕsi*. They were supposed to be versed in magic, and to have a secret which enabled them to govern this metal.[1] They were also makers of *k. pichit*, q.v. These *pandai* were often made Governors of Provinces.

The manufacture of arms was brought to its highest degree of perfection in the reign of the second prince of Majapahit, A.D. 1300: when the first damascened *kĕris* (*k. bĕrpamor*) were made by the *pandai bĕsi* from Pajajeram.

The older *kĕris majapahit* seem to have been made by welding together small bars of iron, like knitting needles, so that the *pamor* resembled hair.

This I think explains the story that the hair of the girl dedicated to the *kĕris* can be seen in the blade.[2] As a matter of fact the hair-like structure usually extends through the hilt. The early *pandai bĕsi* could not make real steel, but found by experiment that iron needles, welded together in this way, were much stronger than plain iron. Later the Arabs taught them to make damascened patterns. (See Plate 5).

According to Malay tradition a *kĕris* must be made of at least two kinds of iron, and a good *kĕris* of seven kinds. The *kĕris* of Hang Tuah, the hero of Malacca history, was of twenty kinds, and these had been obtained from many places, from Bali to Stamboul.

As I have mentioned elsewhere, iron was at one time a rare and therefore costly metal. It played a great part in sorcery and was at one time regarded as talismanic: *sumpah minum ayer bĕsi* means to take an oath by drinking water in which iron has been placed.

K. bĕrpamor is a *kĕris* with a damascened blade. The word *pamor* means alloyed or mixed; and indicates that the iron is mixed with nickel, hence meteoric.

Iron seems to have been known first in Java in the meteoric form, whence its rarity and supposed talismanic value, as shown in the cult of certain early weapons. At a later date when purer iron (*bĕsi khersani*) was imported in ships from the Persian Gulf, a certain amount of meteoric iron was still worked up in the *kĕris* to give magical properties,

---

[1] See Pawang Salleh's story of the making of the *k. majapahit*, p. 32.

[2] See *Legends and Superstitions*.

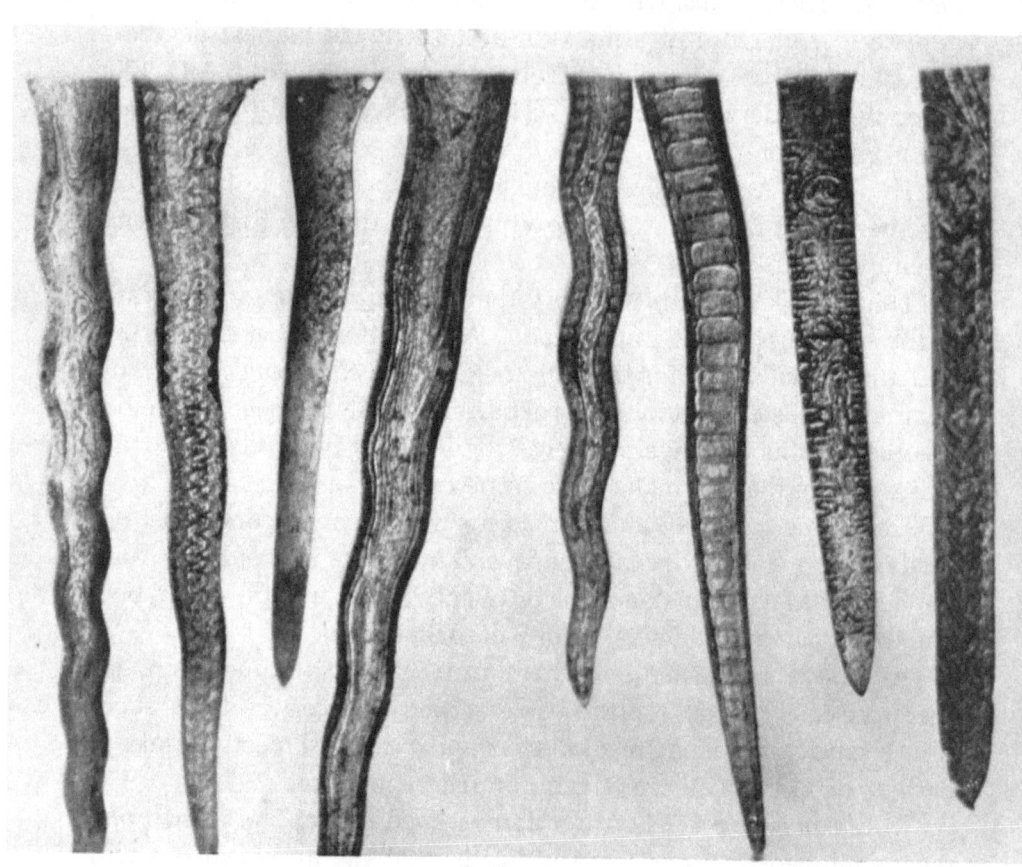

5. *Kĕris* blades showing *pomor*.

the magic coming out in lucky marks, *bunga pamor,* made by the nickel. Much later, in Java, the makers of *kĕris* had enough control of their materials to make ornamental damasks. Indeed damask now can be made by the use of pure nickel, but this lacks the *tuwah* or talismanic virtue attaching to the meteoric iron.

Newbolt writing about 1800 says *bĕsi pamor,* damasked iron, was brought from the Celebes and Java and mixed with the iron from old hoops, nails and a sort of iron from Billiton, one-fourth of the *bĕsi pamor* to three-fourths of the other iron. He also says that the art of inlaying a *kĕris* with gold was no longer known in Malacca, but in Palembang, Siak, Pontianak and Trĕngganu there were able workers in this craft.

The Malay smith's tools are simple, but he can do very clever work with them. He uses a forge, an anvil, hammers, chisels and files, also a characteristic tool called *lepa*. This is a cold chisel fixed at right angles in a long handle.

To make a *kĕris* he first makes a number of small bars. There is always a central plate of steel, that in the finished *kĕris* forms the edge. On each side of this is a layer of *bĕsi pamor* made of iron bars welded together, then beaten into a sort of Greek key pattern (see Plate 6 No. 2). It is then covered with a piece of mild steel. These plates are welded together. Two or more pieces shaped in one of the forms shown in Plate 6 Nos. 4, 5 & 6, are welded on to the hilt end of the weapon.

A piece is now cut off this end with the *lepa* and part of the hilt end is beaten up to form a tang. The cut-off piece is formed into a guard and punched to receive the tang, and welded in place.

The blade of the *kĕris* is now shaped. If the *kĕris* is to be wavy (*bĕrlok*) it is bent. The blade is heated, the parts which are not to be bent are rapidly water-cooled, then the blade is placed edgeways the ends supported by blocks, and is hammered on the uncooled portions.

A separate heating and hammering is needed for each wave. In some *kĕris* especially those made in Patani, the waves are made by filing and grinding, but usually only in *kĕris mĕlela* or *bĕsi bari*[1] as the beauty of the *pamor* is spoilt if it does not follow the waves.

The blade is now ground or filed to its final shape. In the process the outer layer of mild steel is removed and the *kĕris* blade is then tempered.

---

[1] *bari*. I cannot trace this word. In Kĕlantan, Mr. Gardner found it in verbal use. I have not seen it written. The meaning is said to be 'rough.' (BLM)

The *kĕris* blade is next laid in a trough containing boiling rice water, sulphur and salt, for three or four days. This blackens the steel but scarcely touches the iron. It attacks the marks of the welds, which show as tiny etched lines. When this damascened pattern is clear, the blade is cleaned with lime juice.

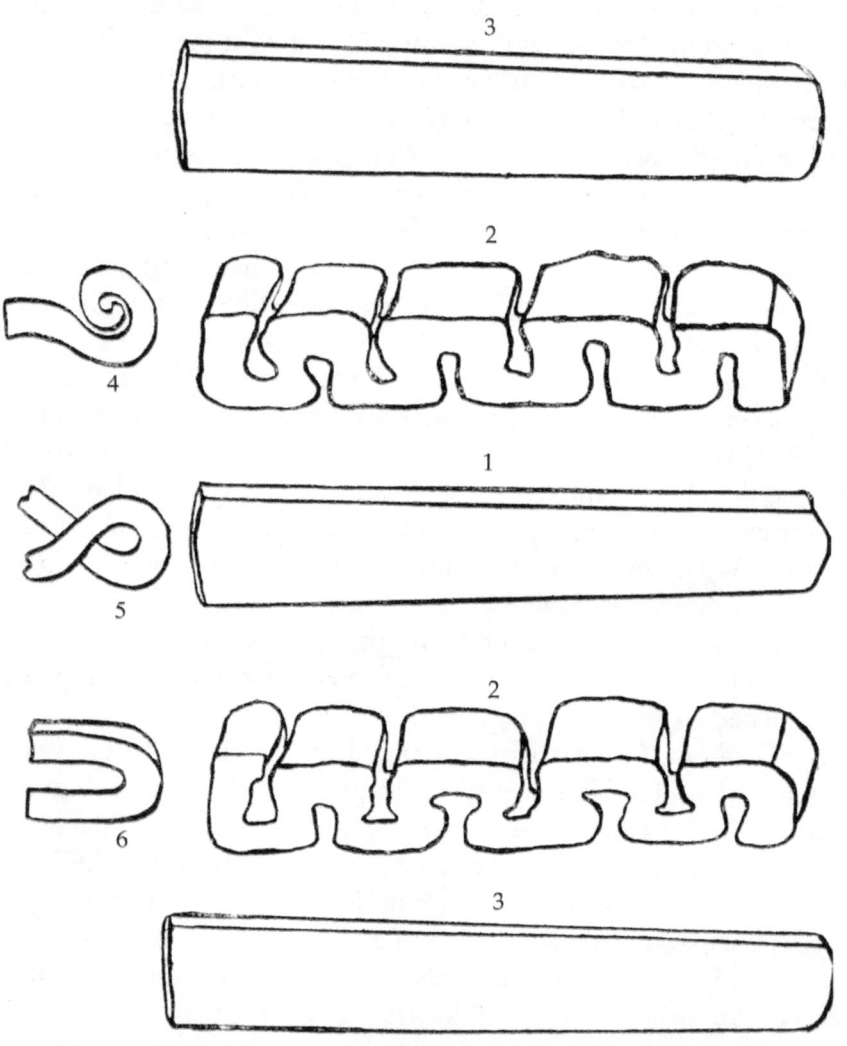

6. The making of a *kĕris* blade.
1. Central plate of steel which forms edge of finished weapon. 2. Bars of *bĕsi pamor* welded on either side of No. 1. 3. Bars of steel welded on either side of the 1 & 2 combination. 4, 5 & 6. Bars of *bĕsi pamor* welded on top to form guard.

CHAPTER 1: KĚRIS

7. Balinese *kěris* hilts.

8. Balinese *kěris* hilts.

IV. THE HILT.

The blade is fixed into the hilt by forcing the hot tang into the hole prepared for it, and filled with glue (*jabong*) made of damar and oil. In modern days gramophone records, crushed and melted, are used, or a piece of rag is twisted around the tang: but in the latter case the *kĕris* is not fit for use

A *kĕris* hilt is usually of wood, but metal, ivory or bone are also used (see Plate 9).

Most *kĕris* have hilts carved in the shape of figures. Since all old *kĕris* that are *bertuwah* are thought to have an indwelling spirit (*sĕmangat*)[1] I fancy that a carved hilt would be considered more or less likely to please this spirit. Now Islam forbids the making or use of images; and as the influence of Islam grew, the use of images was discouraged; but the feeling was that they were lucky, and so, disguised enough to fulfil the letter of the law, they were still used.

Plate 11 No. 6 shows a Malay *kĕris* hilt where the figure is very distinct, but has no face. This omission is probably from religious motives, since, as it had no face it had not the image of a living thing: at the same time it had a body to be inhabited by a *sĕmangat*.

Some *kĕris*, especially those made in Bali and Madura, have most beautifully carved figures and hilts. These may be of wood, ivory, gold, silver or iron. The figures are usually grotesque, of the *wayang kulit* type.

A *kĕris* with a gold hilt is called *k. ulu kĕnchana, k. harubi, k. mĕrubi* or *k. bawang sa-bongkol*. The Sultans of Malacca made a law that only people of royal blood might have gold hilted *kĕris*, but as in later times this law was not observed, a gold sheath was substituted as the distinctive sign of royalty.

A metal cup on the hilt of a *kĕris* is called *pĕndongkok* (see Plate 16 No. 2).

There are many types of hilt.
    (1) The *Sundang* (see Plate 10 No. 1)
    (2) The Bali type (see Plate 10 No. 3)
    (3) The *jawa dĕmam* or *raja dĕmam* (see Plate 10 Nos. 5 & 10)

---

[1] See p. 46.

CHAPTER 1: KĚRIS

9. *Kěris* hilts
1. Wood. 2. Wood and metal. 3. Silver. 4. Ivory (elephant). 5. Ivory (fish). 6. Bone.

(4) The Patani type (see Plate 10 No. 6)
(5) The Flower or Madura type (see Plate 10 No. 7)
(6) The *majapahit* type (see Plate 10 No. 9)
(7) The Bugis type (see Plate 10 No. 2)
(8) The *bahari* type (see Plate 10 No. 8)

(1) The *Sundang* type.

As the *kĕris* became longer and heavier it was used to slash with and the hilt was changed to give a better grip. Also as Malay weapons are fixed to the hilts with a round tang, which is excellent for thrusting, but not for cutting, one or more silver bands (*sigi*) were put on to prevent the blade turning in the hilt. These are recognised as the distinguishing mark of the *sundang*.

(2) The Bali type.

Many of the *kĕris* from Bali have a figure of a god called Arana or Ravana for the hilt, obviously of Hindu origin. Others that are very old have a figure of a man or god who is obviously naked, almost phallic, and I think most likely this is a god.

(3) The *jawa dĕmam*.

The legend is as follows: A certain raja called his *pandai bĕsi* and ordered him to make a *kĕris* hilt that was unlike any other, or lose his life. The *kĕris* maker could not think what to do, but as night came on, it grew cold and the raja who had fever (*demam*) pulled his *sarong* up, and hugged himself to keep warm. Then the *kĕris* maker carved a hilt in his likeness. That, at any rate is the story; but I think the use of a figure is to give luck to the *kĕris*.

(4) The Patani type: *k. hulu pĕkakak*.

The hilt developed a big head with such a long nose that it has been mistaken for a kingfisher, but it is really intended to be human, and there will often be found tiny arms clasped round the body.

CHAPTER 1: KĚRIS

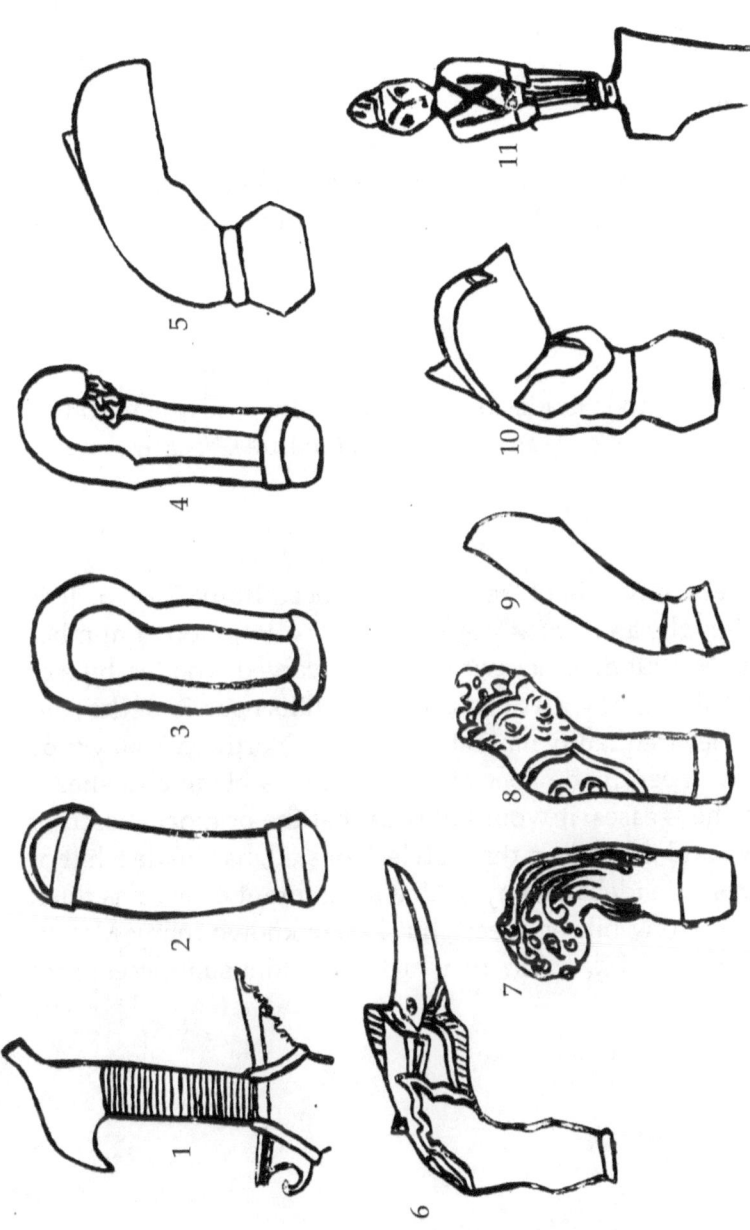

10. *Kĕris* hilts

1. *Sundang*. 2 & 3. Bali type. 4. Javanese type, pistol grip. 5. *Jawa dĕmam* type, Sumatra. 6. Patani type, *hulu pĕkakak*. 7. Madura flower type. 8. *K. bahari*. 9. *Badek* hilt. 10. Northern type, *jawa dĕmam*. 11. Detail of *k. majapahit* hilt.

(5) The Flower or Madura type.

In the Javanese Flower type is often found a little head and arms. Sometimes only eyes and hair are shown.

(6) The *majapahit*.

This is the earliest type of *kĕris* known, and has a hilt in the shape of a little man or god. Hilt and blade are forged from a single piece of iron.

(7) The Bugis type.

This is very plain, and is made so that the *kĕris* can easily be used like a dagger (see Plate 10 No. 2) as well as with the true *kĕris* grip.

(8) The *bahari* type.

The hilt of the k. *bahari* is of horn, usually beautifully carved. It is sometimes, though rarely, of silver, or fish ivory. In Johore a number of these are to be found, either with rough uncarved wooden hilts of the traditional shape, or with ordinary Malay hilts usually of the *jawa dĕmam* type. They frequently have sheaths of the Northern Malay type but which have been made specially for them, as blade and sheath fit exactly. In these cases, it would appear that the original sheath or hilt has rotted, and the owner, through lack of skill, has made a hilt or sheath after his own ideas. It may be that an ignorant dealer has fitted a blade with a wrong hilt or sheath but I have known many Malays who cherish ancestral k. *bahari* to which these unusual accessories have been fitted.

CHAPTER 1: KĚRIS

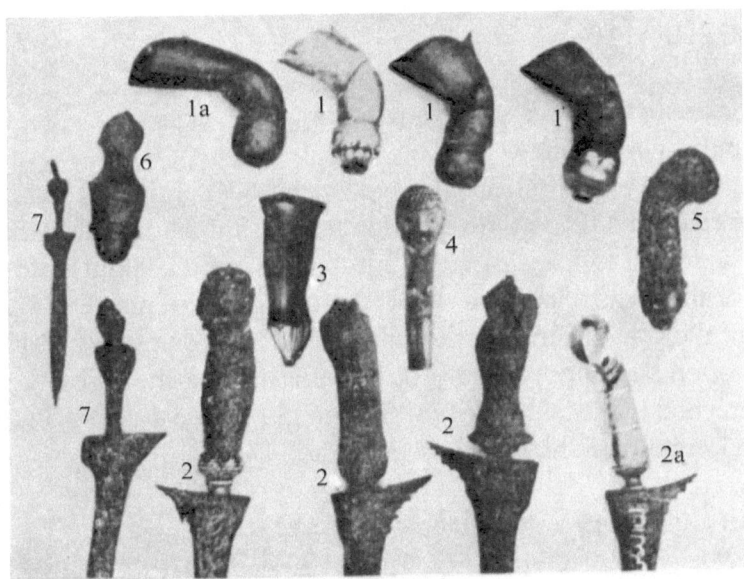

11. *Kěris* hilts.
1. *Jawa děmam*. 1a. *Jawa děmam* (Sumatran). 2. *K. bahari*. 2a. *K. bahari* (silver). 3. Bugis. 4. Javanese. 5. Madura. 6. Malay.

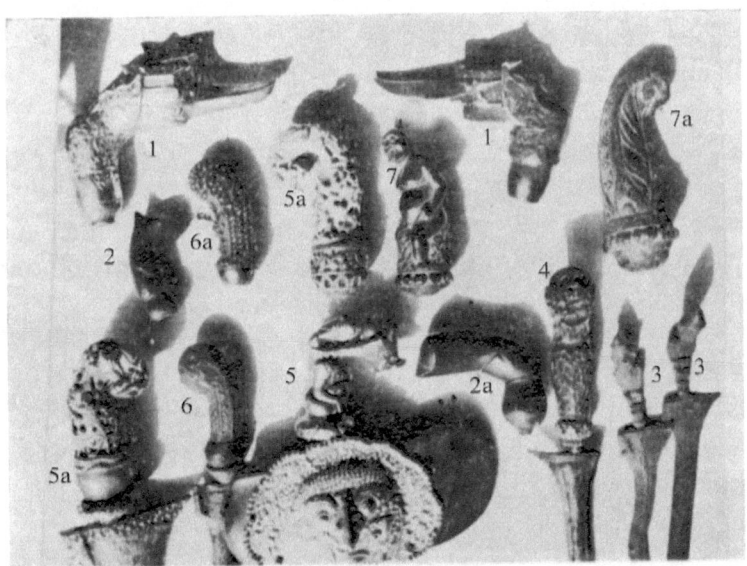

12. *Kěris* hilts.
1. *Hulu pěkakak*. 2. *Jawa děmam*. 2a. *Jawa děmam* (Sumatran). 3. *Majapahit*. 4. *Bahari*. 5. Madura figure type. 5a. Madura flower type. 6. Javanese pistol grip. 6a. Javanese jewel-studded copper-gilt. 7. Balinese figure. 7a. Same as 7, but of carved and painted wood.

V. THE SHEATH.

Sheaths are usually pegged together and glued. Some have the lower part bound with twine.

In modern times the *sampir* often works loose and, catching on the *ganja* comes out with it. One is told that this is intentional, and that the *sampir* is meant to form a guard, but there is not the slightest truth in this. Formerly the *sampir* was kept carefully glued in place, in order to prevent the sheath slipping through the belt and being lost. Formerly a *kĕris* often had a loop of silk cord or *rotan* on the sheath by which it was attached to the belt (*tuli-tuli*). This might have a gold, silver or gilt button loop ornament, *batir-batir* (see Plate 17).

The principal types of sheath are:
    (1) The Northern type.
    (2) The Balinese type.
    (3) The Madura type.
    (4) The *bahari* type.
    (5) The Bugis type.
    (6) The Javanese type.
    (7) The Kĕlantan type.

(1) The Northern type.

This comes from Perak and Malaya generally, had rather a plain cross-piece (*sampir*) with square top edges. The lower end of the sheath (*buntut*) is square and often made of fish ivory.

(2) The Bali type.

The *sampir* and lower end are usually rounded (see Plate 13 Nos. 2 and 3). If the lower part of the sheath (*buntut*) is encased in metal it is called *buntut pĕndok*.

(3) The Madura type.

This often has a round grotesque face on the *sampir* (see Plate 13 No. 3).

CHAPTER 1: KĚRIS

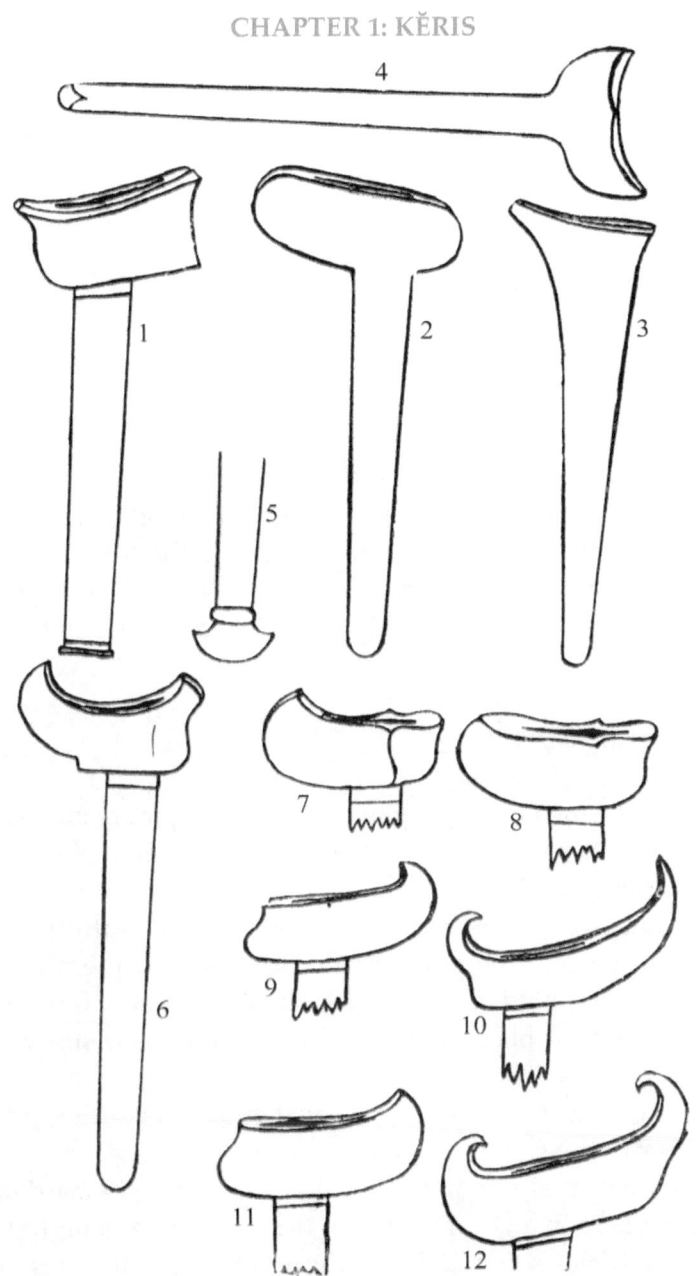

13. *Kěris* sheaths.
1. Northern type; square *sampir* and *buntut*; if *buntut* as No. 5, Bugis.
2. Bali and Madura type.   3. Bali type.   4. *K. bahari*; if cased in silver often has square *buntut* as No. 1.   6. Javanese type.   7, 8, 9, 10 and 11. Javanese. All have rounded *sampir*.   12. Kělantan. Has rounded *buntut* unless cased in silver, when it is square as in No. 1.

(4) The *bahari* type.

The tip is usually rounded (see Plate 13 No. 4) but if cased in silver often has a square tip as in Plate 13 No. 1.

(5) The Bugis type.

See Plate 13 No. 5.

(6) The Javanese type.

This has a flamboyant *sampir* with a rounded tip. It often has the sheath enclosed in metal, sometimes with a slit down the front to show the wood of the sheath. This slit may be filled in with tortoise-shell. If a metal sheath has no slit it is called *buntu*; if it has a slit, *tapeh*; if the slit is closed at the top *sĕlarak*.

(7) The Kĕlantan type.

This is very like the Java type. The tips of the *sampir* are inclined to be more curved. These sheaths are often made of a single piece of wood without a join. (See Plate 15 No. 1).

Many sheaths are encased in silver very beautifully worked. These are often made for sale to Europeans; and there is quite a trade fitting *kĕris* blades with silver sheaths for this purpose. If a weapon has a poor blade, a poorly carved hilt and a silver sheath, avoid it.

To the Malay the blade is the most important thing, then the hilt, and lastly the sheath. If he has the money he will have a good hilt before he puts silver on the sheath. A man may be hard up, and put a poor blade in a good sheath in order to sell at a high price.

Avoid all Malay silver, *kĕris* sheaths or otherwise, that has a design of two crossed *kĕris*, or a *kĕris* and a sheath crossed. That is to catch globe trotters and nearly always made by Chinese, though Kĕlantan Malays have copied it from them in the past few years. They are made to sell only to Europeans.

A gold casing is called *k. tĕrapang* if it only covers the lower part of the sheath leaving the *sampir* exposed; if this is also covered it is called

CHAPTER 1: KĚRIS

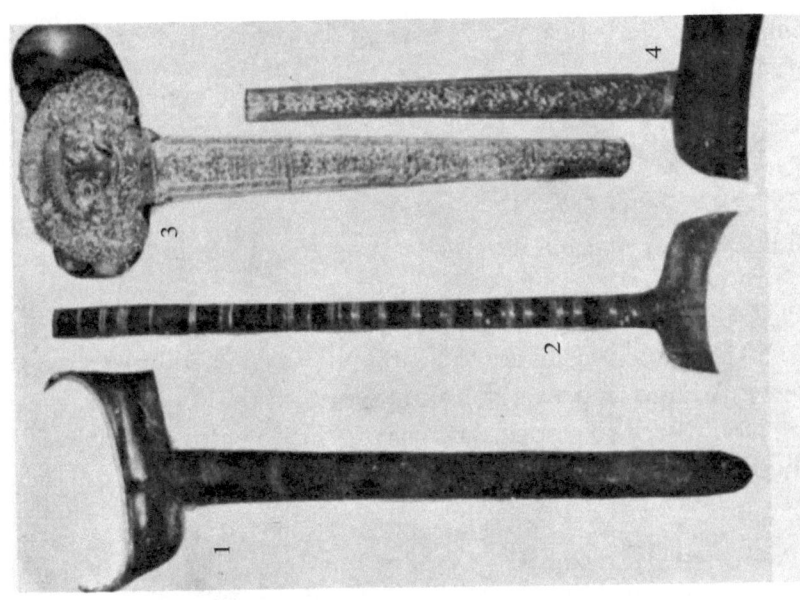

15. 1. Kělantan. 2. K. bahari. 3. Madura. 4. Northern.

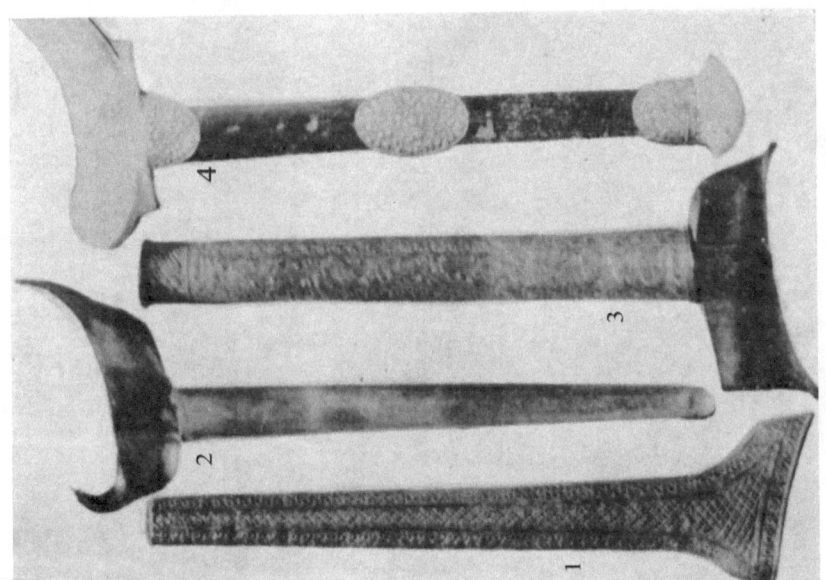

14. 1. Balinese. 2. Javanese. 3. Northern. 4. Bugis

Kěris sheaths.

k. *těrapang gabus*. Gold sheathed *kěris* were the prerogative of royalty in Malacca.

KĚRIS RINGS.

Chinchin mělawan or *chinchin panchar kěnyang*. (See Plate 16 No. 1).

If a *kěris*, especially one of the short hilted type, struck something hard (e.g. a bone) the hand was likely to be injured by contact with the top of the *aring*. A large ring was therefore worn on the forefinger: any large ring would serve but special rings were made with one side very thick. These are becoming rare and are worth collecting.

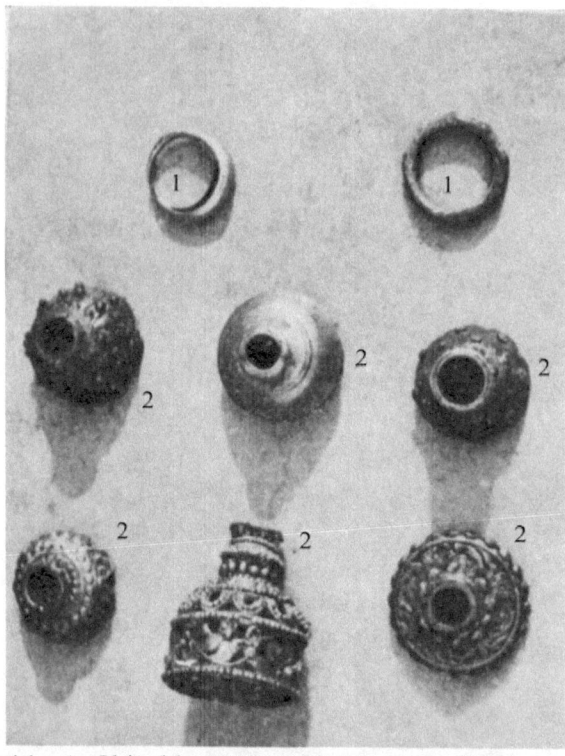

16. 1. *Chinchin mělawan; kěris rings.*
    2. *Pěndongkok.*

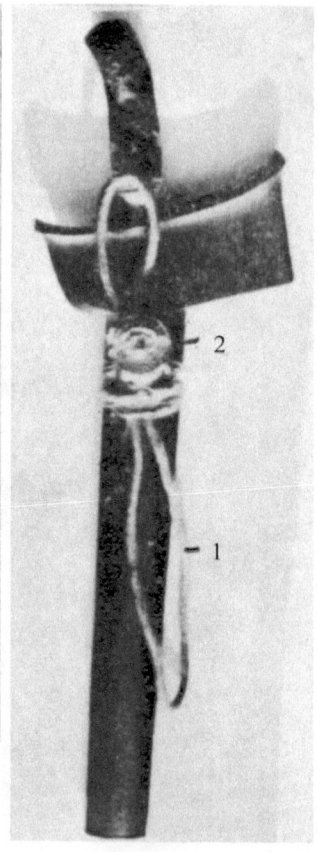

17. 1. *Tuli-tuli.*
    2. *Batir-batir.*

VI. CLASSIFICATION.

One is shown a flimsy fish sting set into a handle, a large sword, a sort of rapier, and various double and single edged daggers and all sorts of intermediate shapes and told that they are all *kĕris*.

It must be remembered that weapons are apt to change in 2,000 years with new methods and wants. English swords have changed as much in the same time, and the various stages in the evolution of the *kĕris* can be clearly seen.

According to Malays there are five classes of *kĕris*.
    a. Those from the Northern States of Malaya and Patani.
    b. Those from Rembau.
    c. Javanese.
    d. Bugis.
    e. Sumatran.

They are said to classify them according to:
    (1) The *pamor*.
    (2) The iron.
    (3) The shape of the blade.
    (4) The hilt.

They recognise however that an old *kĕris* has probably had many hilts in its time.

All Malay weapons if made of metal are divided into three classes, *bĕrpamor* if damascened or laminated, *mĕlela* if plain steel, and *bĕsi bari* if rough steel (like sandpaper).

In practice, the Malays to whom I have shown my 400 *kĕris* seem to be guided by the shape of the hilt and sheath. A *kĕris* with a Javanese hilt was said by one Malay to be Javanese, although six months before he had recognised the same blade as Bugis, because I showed it to him with a Bugis hilt; or Patani, if I showed it to him then with a Patani hilt. Patani *kĕris* with *jawa dĕmam* hilts will be said to be Javanese because the Java and Patani sheaths are very much alike. I have no doubt there are experts who can tell the *kĕris* by the iron, etc., but as each Malay I have consulted during the last thirty years has told me different things about the same *kĕris* I am puzzled.

KERIS AND OTHER MALAY WEAPONS

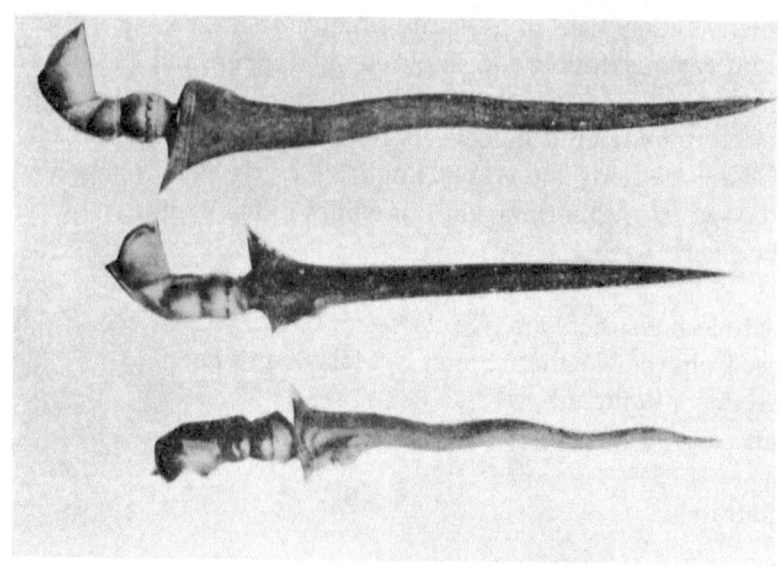

19. Kĕris sĕmpana.

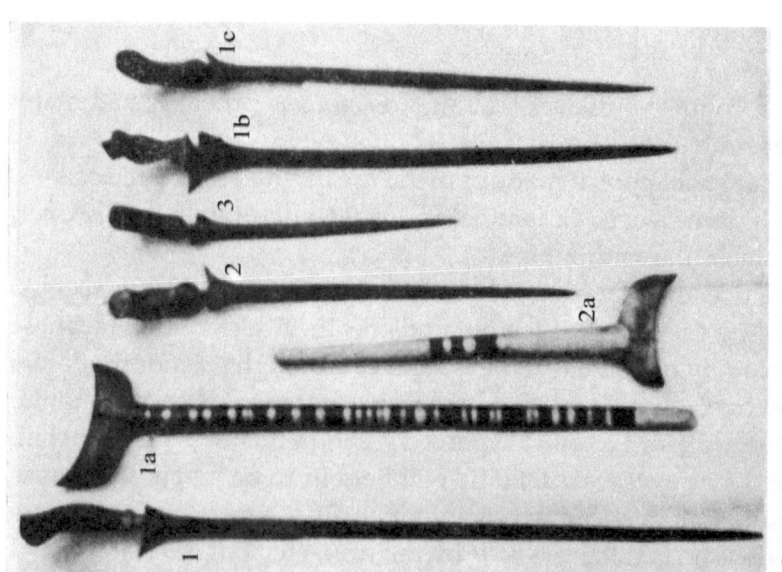

18. 1 & 1a. K. panjang and sheath. 1b & 1c. K. panjang. 2 & 2a. K. alang. 3. K. pendek.

CHAPTER 1: KĚRIS

Many smell a blade saying that they can tell where a *kěris* is made by the smell. Others put it to the ear, and say that the blade will tell where it was made, if the listener has the proper power. They do not ring the blade, but hold it to the ear and listen to the sound they say it makes.

It may be possible for some of them to tell the origin of an individual *kěris* by occult means, but I have tried marking the blades and putting different hilts on, and the answers are always according to the hilt, sheath, etc.

There are said to be masters who will speak to the *kěris* saying in turn all the likely names of the places at which it may have been made and at the proper name the *kěris* will stand up; but I have not yet been able to find such a master.

I think the best way to list *kěris* is as follows:
(1) *Kěris sěmpana*. The ordinary *kěris,* straight or wavy.
(2) *Kěris panjang* or *k. bahari*. The Sumatran rapier *kěris* (execution *kěris*).
(3) *Sundang* (the Malay broadsword).
(4) *Tumbok lada* (pepper crusher) so called from the shape of the hilt.
(5) *Badek*.
(6) *Kěris majapahit,* which is Javanese.
(7) *Kěris pichit* (finger pressed *kěris*).
(8) *Kěris ikan pari*.

(1) This is called by many names: as *kěris sapukul* if straight, *kělok* if wavy. The waves (*lok*) in Malay *kěris* are always uneven in number, every wave on each side is counted: so a *kěris* with a single bend is counted as having three *lok*. If it has three *lok* it is called *kěris sěmpana kěling,* if five or seven, *k. sěmpana* or *k. parong sari*. If nine or more *kěris chěrita*. If a *kěris* has thirteen or fifteen *lok* it is sometimes called *kěris tambang sěrai*.

I have a *kěris* with thirty-one waves, which is the greatest number I have seen, but Leonard Wray[1] speaks of one with forty-seven.

---

[1] Leonard Wray (1852-1942), engineer, author, photographer and ethnographer, spent much of his working life in the colony of Malaya. He contributed a chapter on Malay crafts to Wright & Cartwright's book on British Malaya (see Bibliography). (Ed.)

KERIS AND OTHER MALAY WEAPONS

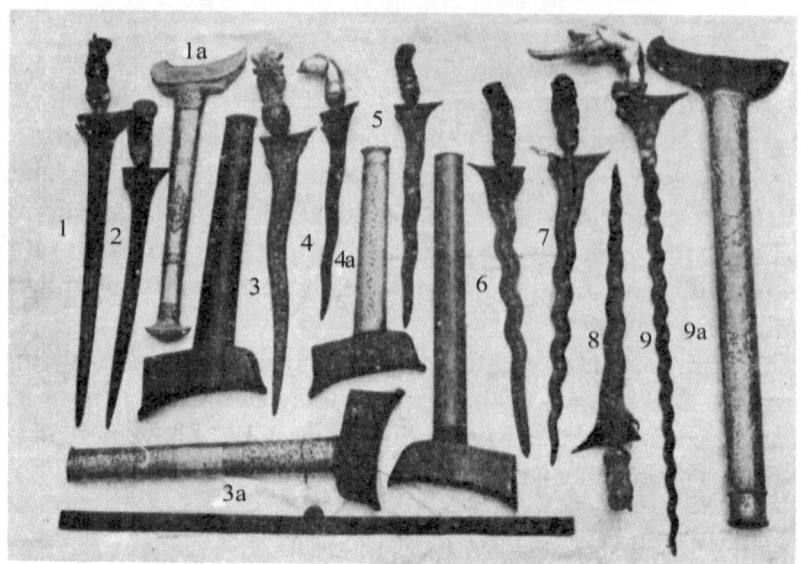

20. 1 & 1a. Straight *kĕris* and sheath.   2. Same as 1.   3 & 3a. *K. sĕmpana kĕling* and sheath.   4 & 4a. *Kĕris* of 5 waves and sheath: *k. sĕmpana* or *k. parong sari*.   5. *Kĕris* of 7 waves, names as 4.   6. *Kĕris* of 9 waves: *k. chĕrita*.   7. *Kĕris* of 13 waves: *k. tambang sĕrai*.   8. *Kĕris* of 15 waves, name as 7. 9. *Kĕris* of 31 waves.

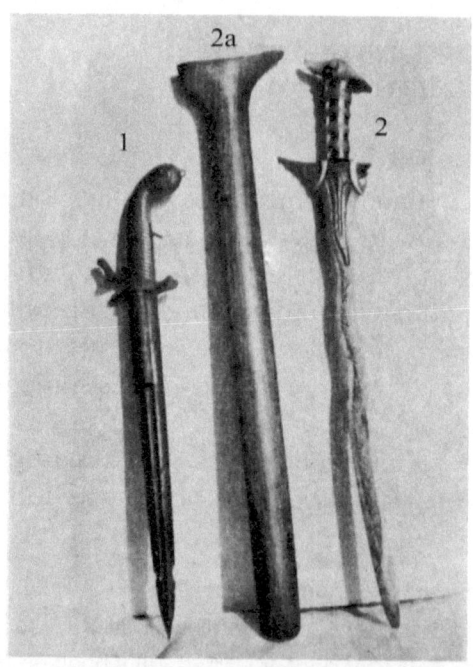

21. 1. *Kĕris* with pistol barrels (see text).   2 & 2a. *Sundang* and sheath.

CHAPTER 1: KĔRIS

(2) *K. panjang* or *k. bahari.*

This is a Sumatran rapier *kĕris* called the execution *kĕris*. If long it is called *k. panjang,* if medium *k. alang,* and if short *k. pendek.*

It has a characteristic hilt (see Plate 18) and one can usually be certain that it comes from either Sumatra or Mĕnangkabau, the people of which are Sumatran. It was made primarily for fighting and was used only incidentally for executions.

The usual Malay mode of execution was *salang* or slaying with a *kĕris*.[1] The victim was made to squat and the executioner drove the *k. panjang* from a certain spot (*tĕmpat penggalan*) inside his collar bone down into his heart. This execution was carried out quickly or slowly according to the sentence. The *kĕris* was driven through cotton wool so that the blood was soaked up, since only the ruler could cause blood to be shed.[2]

(3) *Sundang.*

The *sundang* is two edged and may be straight or sinuous. It has the *ganja, aring,* and other features of the *kĕris* but has its own peculiar type of hilt and has almost lost its point. It has the *lambai gajah* and *Bĕlalai gajah* q.v. (See Plate 21 No. 2). In the Philippines it is simply called a *kĕris*.

(4) *Tumbok lada.*

The *tumbok lada* has a slightly curved blade, with a single edge on the concave side of the blade. The hilt is always in the same plane as the blade instead of at right angles to it, as with the true *kĕris*.

It is intended primarily for stabbing, as is a *kĕris* proper, but is also used as a knife. It is usually from six to ten inches long, but I have specimens eighteen inches long. (See Plate 22 No. 3).

---

[1] Another method of execution was strangling (*kujut*) with a cord or bow-string. The term *kujut* is sometimes used for hanging by pulling the body upwards instead of in the modern way of breaking the neck by the drop.

[2] Executions were sometimes carried out by blowing from a gun, *bunoh di-mulut mĕriam.*

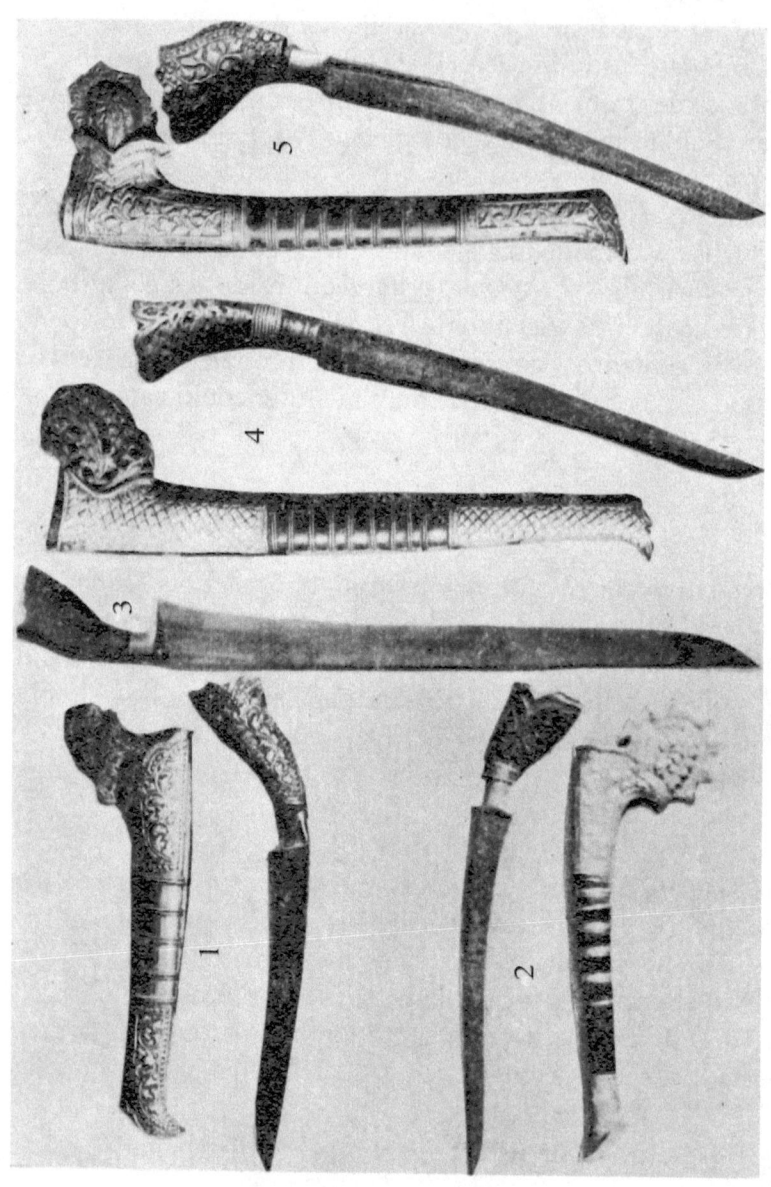

22. Tumbok lada.
1, 2, 4 & 5. Silver mounted *tumbok lada* and sheaths. 3. 18 in. *tumbok lada* with wooden handle.

CHAPTER 1: KĚRIS

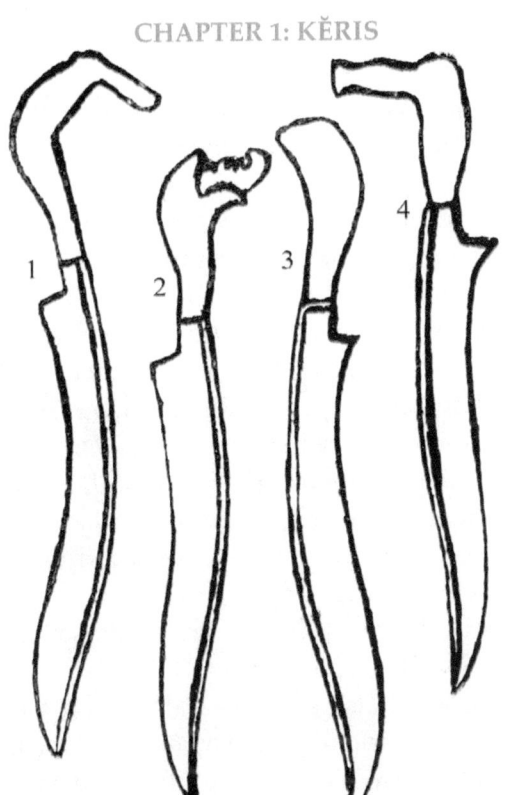

23. 1 & 2. *Renchong acheh*. 3. *Sewar*. 4. *Renchong*.

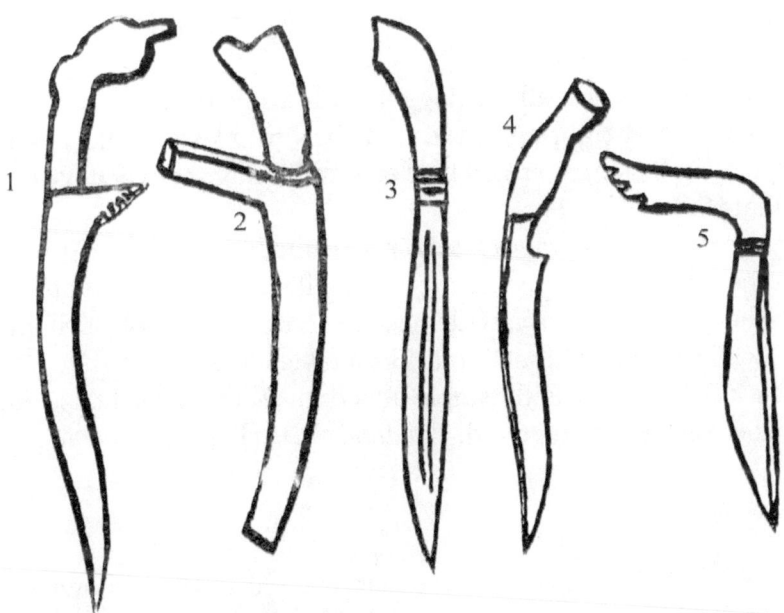

24. 1. Sumatran *sewar*. 2. Sumatran *sewar* in sheath. 3. Sumatran *badek*.
4. Sumatran *sewar*. 5. Javanese *badek*.

The hilt is distinctive and is usually thought to give it its name. *Tumbok* means to crush or pound. Some people say that the shape of the hilt resembles the pestle used to crush pepper corns; others say that the victim when stabbed in the stomach with a *tumbok lada,* has a burning sensation as if he had eaten pepper. I think this is perhaps an understatement.

In Patani, a *tumbok lada* is called a *badek.* Also many Malays shown a knife the name of which they do not know will call it *badek.*

In Mĕnangkabau and Negri Sembilan where the wearing of the *kĕris* is limited to the major chiefs, the *tumbok lada* is the ceremonial weapon of minor chiefs. In Perak and Selangor it is smaller and rather despised as a woman's weapon, 'a pepper crusher,' and associated with underhand blows, being easily hidden and used unexpectedly against the softer parts of the body.

Sewar: a *tumbok lada* with a different hilt but used in the same way, i.e. for thrusting. (See Plates 23 & 24).

The *renchong acheh* is also a *tumbok lada* with a different hilt. It is also worn as a dress weapon in places where a *kĕris* would not usually be worn; but it can be used with great effect as a ripping knife. (See Plate 23).

(5) *Badek.*

This type of *kĕris* is really a dagger with a hilt in the plane of the blade, and not at right angles to it, as in a true *kĕris*. It has a small, straight, usually single-edged blade, with a straight or concave edge. (See Plate 26).

It differs from the *tumbok lada* in that the blade is of even width, while the *tumbok lada* tapers to the point. The hilt, also, is of a different type. The *tumbok lada* has a wide back in section like an old-fashioned razor, while the *badek* in section is like a table knife.

The *badek* while usually single edged has sometimes a false edge, and is occasionally two-edged. The *tumbok lada* has only one edge.

(6) *K. majapahit.*

The type called *majapahit* is the earliest metal *kĕris* known. The traditional form is a straight narrow thin blade of black iron.

CHAPTER 1: KĚRIS

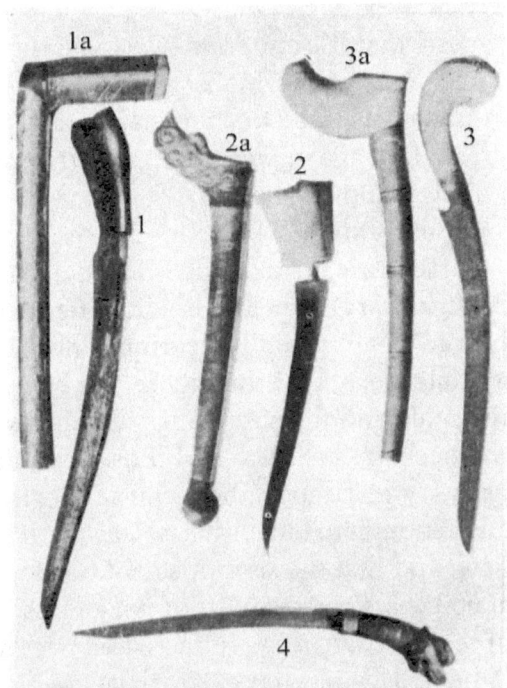

25. 1 & 1a. *Sewar.* 2 & 2a. Sumatran *tumbok lada* and sheath. 3 & 3a. *Renchong Acheh* and sheath. 4. *Sewar.*

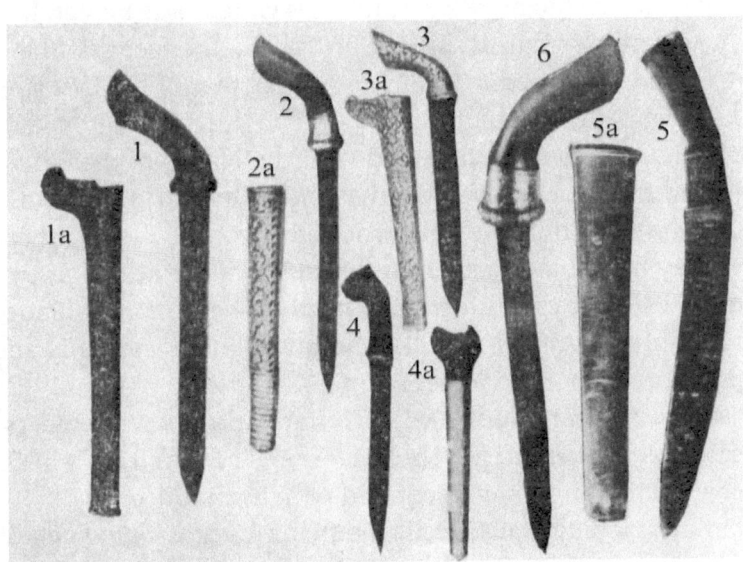

26. 1 & 1a. *Badek* (*old*) and sheath. 2 & 2a. Silver mounted *badek* and sheath. 3 & 3a. Silver hilted *badek* and sheath. 4. Unusual type of hilt and sheath. 5 & 5a. Old *badek* and sheath. 6. *Badek*

The name suggests that it came from Majapahit in Java, the little state that conquered most of the Malay world in the 13th century; but Dr. van Stein Callenfels, the Dutch archaeologist, tells me that it belongs to the earliest iron age in Java about the 7th century A.D. and that scarcely anything is known about it.

Malay writings say it should be shaped like, and as thin as, a blade of *lalang* (coarse grass). The blade and guard are forged of a single piece of iron (*ganja iras*). The hilt is a little figure of a man with a more or less bowed head, usually wearing a hat or some sort of headdress. Some Malays say that this figure can be male or female, the big ones being male and the small ones females; others say that those showing the necklace are male and those without, female. All agree that they are very poisonous, the usual saying is, 'the depth of the white of a nail is enough to kill with a *majapahit*.' It is said that the poison is in the iron and that the *kĕris* does not need to be poisoned. It is possible that 600 years' rust is in itself poisonous.

Some of them seem to date from a time when iron was a rare and precious thing. I have several whose length averages 4¾ inches of which the blade is 1¼ inches and the handle is 1½ inches. They range from this up to 10 inches in length.

When iron became more plentiful *kĕris* were made bigger; but that all early *kĕris* were small is, I think proved by the fact that the name of Sang Puna is recorded in Malay history as that of the first smith to make *kĕris* 3½ palms in length.

Some are quite heavy and sturdy but the blades of the older ones are thin and flimsy. However, used as the *k. ikan pari* is used, a quick jab and withdraw, while the poison does the work, they would be very deadly. They must have been used to thrust and withdraw as a rapier is used; any sideways strain would have broken the thin blade as it would that of a *k. ikan pari* q.v. The Malay is quick and agile and the rapier type of weapon is ideal for him.

Kĕris majapahit are supposed to bring luck to their owners, but some say a *kĕris majapahit* is only lucky if it is acquired by inheritance or by chance; that luck is not acquired with a bought *kĕris*.

A famous *pawang*, Salleh, tells me that a *k. majapahit jantan* (male) was made by a male smith. When finished it was tempered by being made red hot and cooled by being drawn under his armpit, then thrown forward into water. A *k. majapahit pĕrĕmpuan* (female) was made

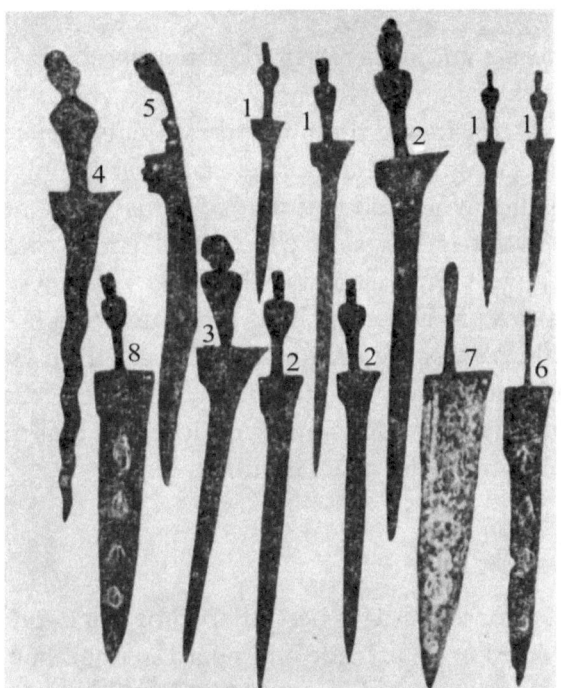

27. Early *k. majapahit*. 2. Slightly later *k. majapahit*. 3. Later and heavier *k. majapahit*. 4. Later and sinuous blade. 5. Unusual variant. 6. Early *k. pichit*. 7. Later *k. pichit*. 8. *Pichit* with *majapahit* hilt (possibly a forgery).

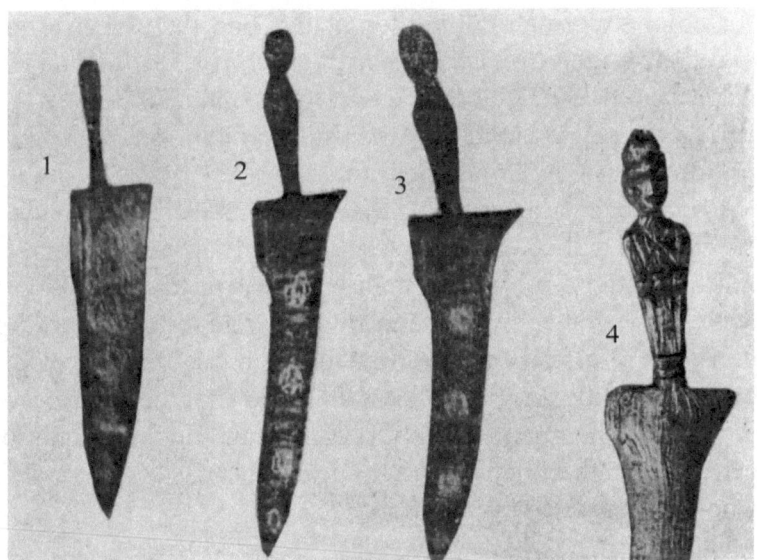

28. 1. Rare type *k. pichit*. 2 & 3. Trěngganu forgeries of *majapahit-pichit*. 4. Detail of *majapahit* hilt.

by a female *pandai* and received its final tempering, by being drawn between her *vulva* and thrown backwards into water. The *pandai* are unhurt which is considered proof that they are real *pandai*.

It is generally agreed that a *kĕris majapahit* is only lucky if the *sĕmangat* likes the owner and that the *kĕris* must be treated with great respect. K. *majapahit* are also said to banish all fear; to confer immunity from jungle dangers since elephant, tiger and *sĕladang* will turn tail if such a *kĕris* is drawn. Other qualities attributed to a k. *majapahit* are: that it will rattle (*kolak-kalek*) in its sheath to warn the owner of danger; that it will guide the hand when fighting; and even that it will jump out of the hand and fight of its own volition; and that the wearing of such a *kĕris* will render its owner invulnerable.[1]

(7) *Kĕris pichit*.

This is a *kĕris* supposed to have been shaped by finger pressure. Like k. *majapahit* it is *ganja iras* (i.e. blade and guard in one) though the guard is so small as to be negligible. These *kĕris* exist in numbers. They are all very broad and thin, having dents on one side, and slight corresponding bumps on the other; these are exactly the shape and size of finger marks. It is as if they had been made of wax and had been pinched with finger and thumb down the blade. Malays believe that certain *pandai*, saints, kings or other super-naturally gifted beings had the power to mould iron with their fingers. '*Jikalau běsi pun di-pichit-nya, měnjadi lilin.*' 'Were it steel and he pinched it, it became wax in his hand.'

'Suru' is the name ascribed to the traditional maker.

On examining k. *pichit* it is clear that the blade has been made first in the ordinary way; it is probable that the dents were then made with a round headed punch. On the other hand the iron is so thin, that I believe it is quite possible for a man who was used to working with that metal, and whose thumbs and fingers were hardened to dip his hands in oil and quickly pinch these dents in. Such a feat would be no more wonderful than firewalking. It is said that many professional conjurors use on their hands a mixture of camphor and styrax dissolved in spirit, and can then handle red hot iron with ease. The *pandai* may have known some such preparation.

[1] See Invulnerability, p. 114.

CHAPTER 1: KĚRIS

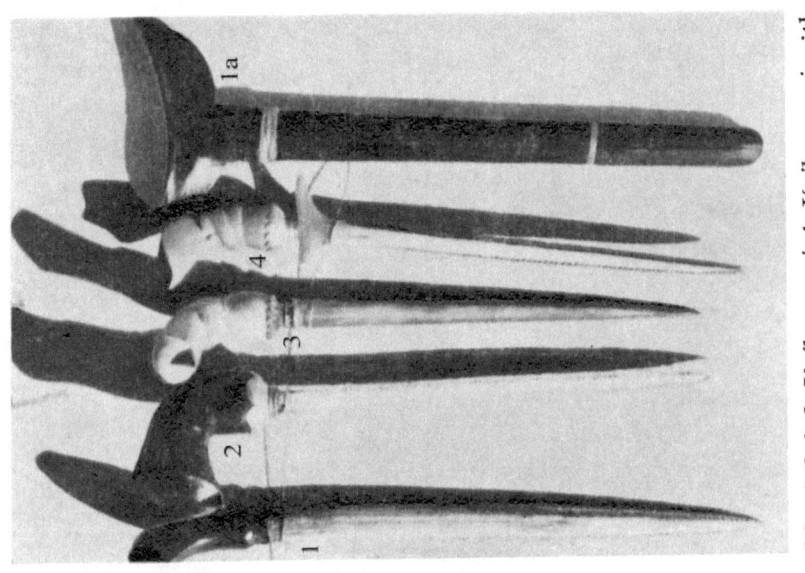

30. 1, 2 & 3. K. *ikan pari*. 4. K. *ikan pari* with *ganju* of horn. 1a. Sheath of No. 1.

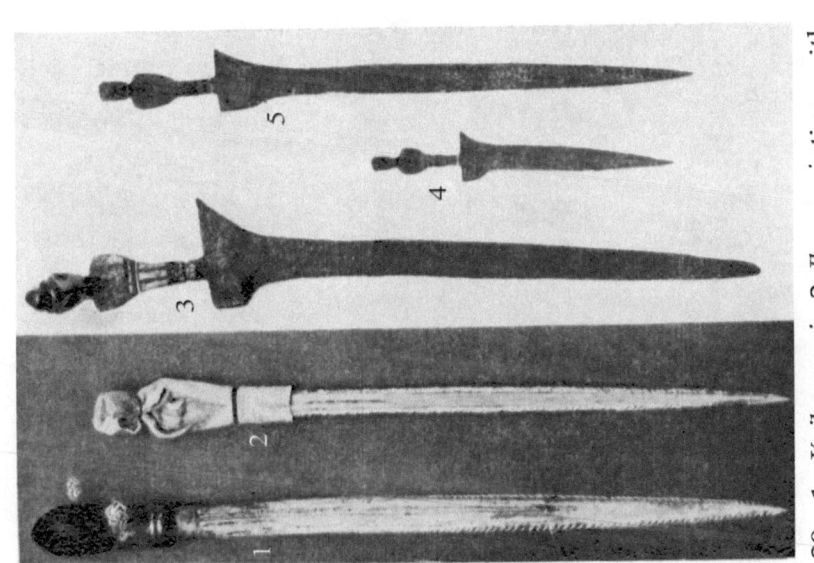

29. 1. K. *ikan pari*. 2. *Ikan pari sting*, with cloth handle. 3, 4 & 5. K. *majapahit*.

Out of ten *k. pichit* I have only two that are thick enough to be used as *kĕris;* the others, being not much thicker than tin, would bend if used with any force, so I conclude that they were used principally as talismans; but of course they may have been poisoned and used in the same way as *k. majapahit* and *k. ikan pari,* q.v.

K. majapahit showing *pichit* marks are known but I believe these are Javanese, made after 1500 A.D. There are also imitations of the above with thick heavy blades and all sorts of lucky marks (including *pichit*) hammered in, which come from Trĕngganu. (See Plate 28 Nos. 2 & 3).

(8) *Kĕris ikan pari.*

The *k. ikan pari* which, I have stated elsewhere, is probably the origin of all *kĕris,* is so good that in modern times it is still used and valued highly. Dr. Gimlette in his book: *Malay Poisons and Charm Cures,* speaks of it as being used in assassinations, and I have been told that it is still often used in the north with lethal effect; since two or three of the barbs remain in the flesh, carrying the poison with them.

When examining a specimen that is known to have killed a man, I removed the hilt and found the blade sharpened to facilitate its insertion in the hilt, exactly resembling a ray sting, pointed at each end, which was discovered in the excavations at Sĕlinsing, Pĕrak. (See *Journal F.M.S. Museums* 1932 *Plate* XLI *fig.* 2). The people of Sĕlinsing lived in the 6th century. They knew iron and could make wooden handles. I have no doubt this was a *kĕris,* the handle of which had rotted away.

31. *Kěris naga*, showing dragon's body and head. Inscription shows it as having belonged to Sultan Muzaffar Shah of Malacca. (XV. century).

VII. VARIOUS.

A single *kĕris* may be of several varieties; in fact, to name some *kĕris* correctly is like the blazoning of a coat of arms by a herald. For instance, if a *kĕris* blade is set at a slight angle to its hilt, it may be called *k. jalar jantan* (see Plate 38 Nos. I & 3). This *kĕris* is also *k. sĕmpana kĕling, k. bĕrpamor, k. hulu gading, k. jawa dĕmam* (because of its hilt) and *k. sigi* because of the metal bands on its sheath.

Among Javanese varieties are:
  K. *bĕrjol*, a plain, short and straight Javanese *kĕris*.
  K. *pasupati*, a small bladed *kĕris* carried by women. According to Javanese legends, Saputram, the first King of Java, was said to have been born with one of these *kĕris* in his hand or by his side.
  K. *choban*, having twin grooves down the blade near the hilt, bearing a needle like projection down the centre. This is found also in Kĕlantan *kĕris*. Often in old *kĕris* of this type the grooves have rusted through, as in Plate 38 No. 4; in this case the *kĕris* is usually said to have become *bĕrtuwah* (lucky).
  A *kĕris* with a large *aring* is Javanese.

From the Northern Malay States and Patani come the following:
  K. *bĕsi bari*, a *kĕris* without *pamor* but with a rough surface like sandpaper.

In Kĕlantan also they make a *kĕris* with a straight groove down the centre of each side, no *pamor* and a number of waves (made by grinding and not by bending). It seems to have no particular name.

From Patani comes the *k. ulu pĕkakak*, with the kingfisher hilt. According to books this type is also called *k. tĕrajang* because it is often so long that the sheath has to be kicked up and the *kĕris* drawn over the shoulder. I could never get anyone to do this for me, though they had heard of it in Kĕlantan. If worn in the belt this *kĕris* can easily be drawn like a sword; but I suppose in former times there was some trick in drawing it over the shoulder which placed one's enemy at one's mercy. (See Plate 33).

If a straight *kĕris* has no *aring* but is fretted under the *silang* or pointed at the end of the *ganja* it is peninsular. (See Plate 40 No. 2).

CHAPTER 1: KĚRIS

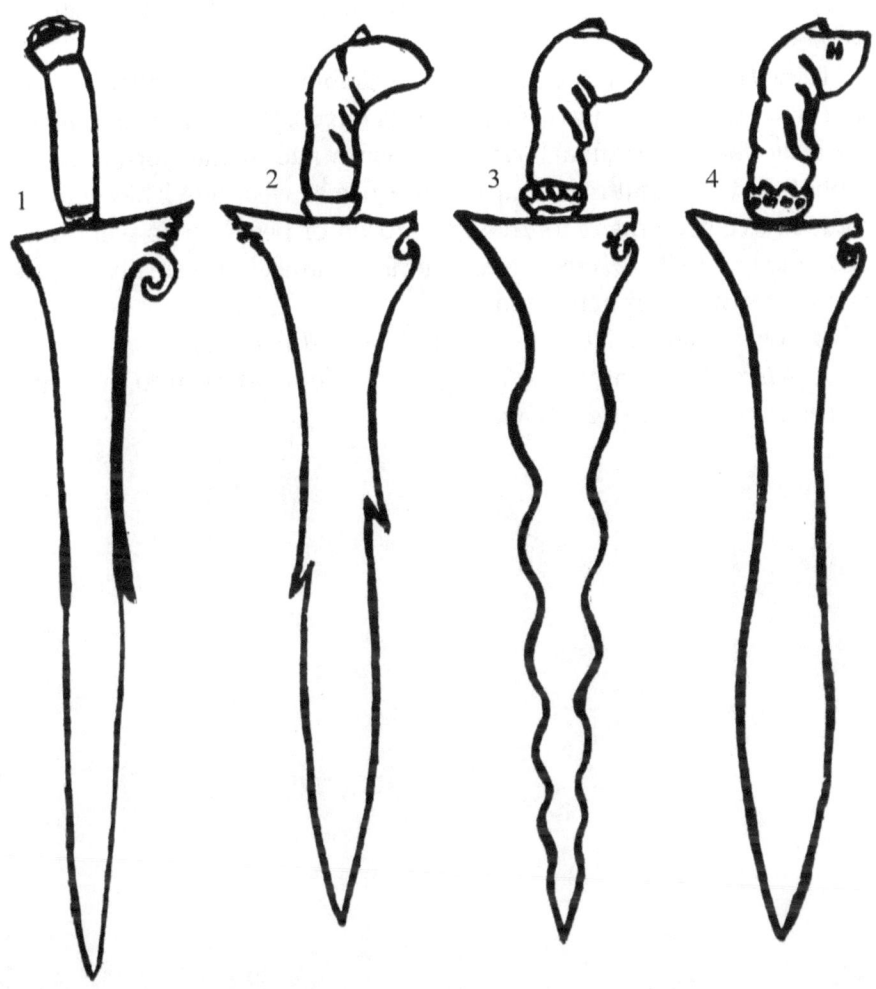

32. 1. Bali *kěris* with false edge and reversed *Bělalai gajah* on pointed side of *ganja*. 2. *Bango dolog* (Javanese). 3. *Bendasegada* (serrated, not sinuous). 4. *Kalamisana*

When the blade and the guard are in one piece the *kĕris* is called *k. ganja iras* but many *kĕris* claimed to be *ganja iras* are ordinary *kĕris* that have lost their *ganja*. (See Plate 38 No. 2).

Daga is a small *kĕris* used in the Philippines, it has a guard instead of a *ganja*. The name comes from the English word 'dagger.' (Plate 39 No. 7).

If the *kĕris* has a rounded point like a table knife it is called *k. buah bĕka* or *k. buah bungkal* (rare) (see Plate 34 No. 2). Practically all *sundang* are *buah bĕka* but ordinary *kĕris* are also made in that form, why, I cannot find out, as it must impair their use as weapons. They may of course have been made to give to children or people who were mad and who had to have *kĕris* as a ceremonial adjunct but were given ones that would not do much damage.

If trowel shaped, a *kĕris* is called *k. sudu bĕkang* (rare).

K. tĕtĕrapan has a hollow along the blade to let air into the veins and so make a more deadly wound.

CHAPTER 1: KĔRIS

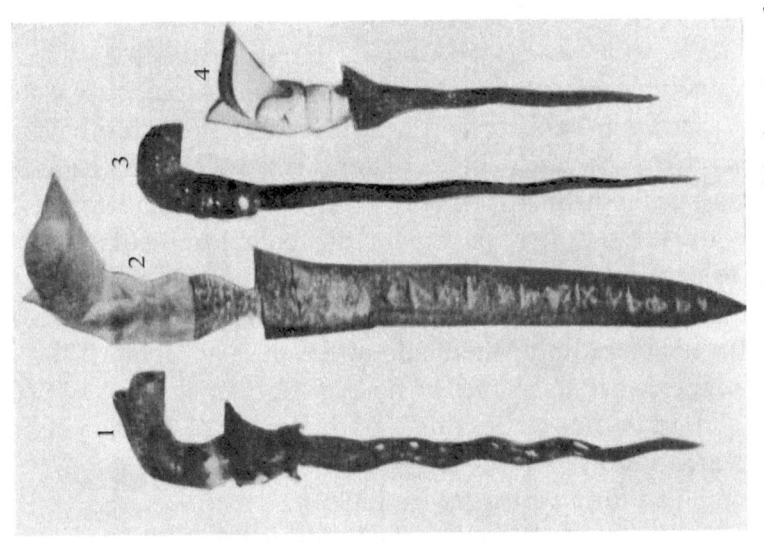

34. 1. *K. sĕmpana*, bronze blade pierced.
2. Heavy bladed *kĕris*: blade incised with cabalistic signs.
3. Stiletto-shaped *kĕris* without *ganja*.
4. Stiletto-shaped *kĕris* with *ganja*.

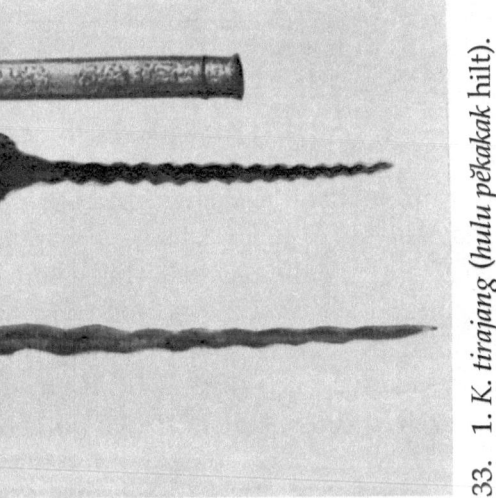

33. 1. *K. tirajang* (*hulu pĕkakak* hilt).
2. The same.   2a. Sheath of No. 2.

VIII. LEGENDS AND SUPERSTITIONS.

There are innumerable superstitions about the *kĕris,* it is impossible to give them all. Certain proportions are considered lucky and to have them is a great virtue in a *kĕris.* There are various ways of testing this.

First by measuring the blade, usually with a strip of palm leaf; the total length is measured from *ganja* to point, the palm leaf is cut to this length, then folded exactly in half, and one half length of the blade thus marked on the *kĕris.* The palm leaf is then cut into pieces, each piece being the exact width of the blade at the marked point. If the proportions are perfect there should be no leaf left over; i.e. the width at the centre should be an exact multiple of the length of the blade. If there is less than a third of a piece left over, the *kĕris* is fairly good, if there is more than a third, it is *chĕlaka* (unlucky).

Another way is to fold the length of the leaf into three and measure the blade at one-third from the point in the same way. After making either of these tests, the slips are put on the floor in the form of a *kĕris.* If they appear as in Plate 35 No. 1 (i.e. an odd number) the *kĕris* is lucky, but if as in Plate 35 No. 2 (i.e. an even number) the *kĕris* may turn against its owner.

Spears are measured in this way also. The proportions in this case do not matter, but the pieces of the palm leaf are put into the pattern shown in Plate 35 No. 3. Odd numbers are again lucky but in this case a point at each end is good.

For *parang,* swords and cutting weapons generally, the proportions do not matter; but they should be measured and the pieces of leaf arranged as in Plate 35 No. 4. In this case, however, an even number is lucky.

Another way is to measure the *kĕris* into thirds with a palm leaf, and at each third to measure the width of the blade into leaf chanting: '*pĕnyakit, kapitan, pĕrĕmpuan*' (sickness, captain, lady) as a child says: 'Tinker, tailor, soldier, sailor.' This chant is called *sĕloka.* If the measurements end at *pĕnyakit,* it is unlucky; if at *kapitan* it is lucky, as this means strength or success: *Pĕrĕmpuan* mean success with women, but induces weakness. For a warrior *kapitan* at all three points is good. A young buck would like *kapitan* at two points and *pĕrĕmpuan* at the other, as then he would succeed in love and war.

Still another way is the *suka badan,* to find out if the *kĕris* is lucky

CHAPTER 1: KĚRIS

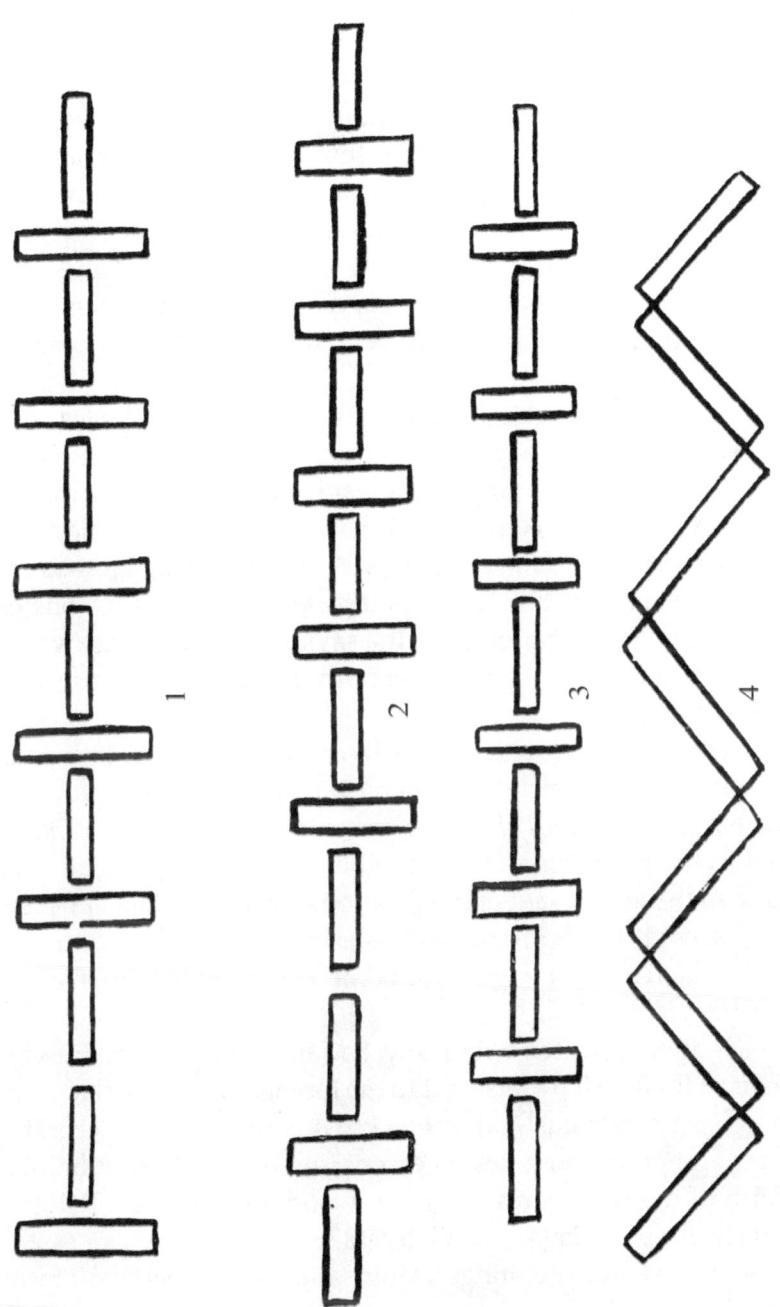

35. Strips of palm leaf arranged for *kěris* measurement (see text).

to a particular person. To do this, he grasps the *kĕris* by the hilt, in the right hand in the stabbing position. He then measures the width of his thumbs at the middle joint alternately, beginning with the left, into the length of the blade. They must fit exactly. With the last thumb he grasps the blade and takes the hilt in his free hand. If the free hand is the right hand, the *kĕris* is lucky for him personally: if the left, the *kĕris* is unlucky and will turn against him. For a left handed man all positions are reversed. This method is used for other weapons, and I have seen it used for guns many times.

Kĕris sometimes have lucky signs carved on the blade. Often these are filled in with gold or silver wire beaten flat and filed smooth. In others they are left unfilled.

These marks may be religious: e.g. the names *Allah* and *Muhammad*, and verses of the *kuran*. They may be lucky or magic verses or magic signs: the seal of Solomon is a favourite, magic squares are also common, but these have usually been miscopied from somewhere since they rarely add up correctly. I have a *kĕris* with five magic squares carved on the hilt and they are all wrong. Is it possible that this is done on purpose? A parallel can be found in the saying of prayers backwards, in order to bring ill luck for someone; or in the loading of a gun with thirteen buckshot.

Oaths are sometimes taken on a *kĕris*: *sumpah minum ayer kĕris*, drinking the water in which a talismanic *kĕris* has been plunged.

Marsden in his *History of Sumatra* says that the value of a *kĕris* is enhanced in the proportion of the number of people it has slain; one that has been the instrument of much bloodshed is regarded almost as something sacred. The horror or enthusiasm inspired by bloodthirsty deeds is transferred to the weapon. Some *kĕris* are distinguished by pompous names.

A *kĕris* is always treated with respect. Many people when drawing an old *kĕris* will salute it by raising it to the forehead. A particularly fine *kĕris* often has its own cushion (*bantal kĕris*) which may be decorated with silver and on which it lies when not in use. In Bali, *kĕris* holders in the form of human figures carved in wood are still used. Religion forbids their use in Malaya. (See Plates 42 & 43).

Malays believe that old things acquire a soul (*sĕmangat*). Wilkinson says that *simangat*, the essence of physical life, must not be confused with the Muslim idea of the soul which lives immortally in Heaven.

CHAPTER 1: KĚRIS

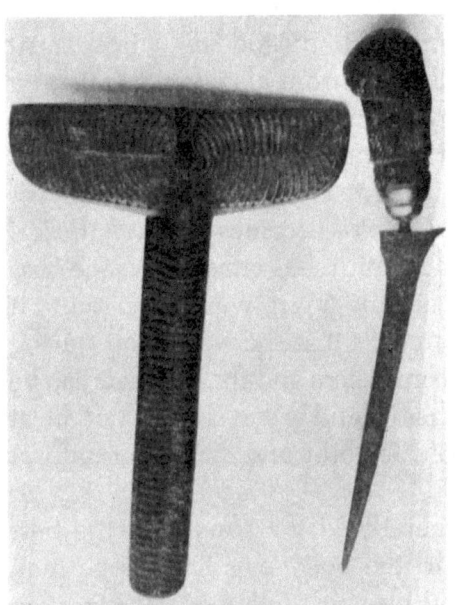

36. Javanese *kěris* and sheath; note large *sampir*.

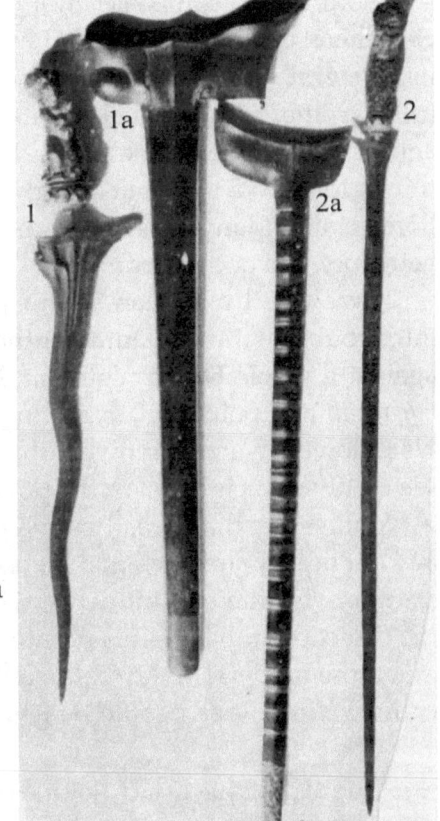

37. 1. Balinese *kěris*, ornate gem studded hilt.
    1a. Sheath of No. 1.
    2. *K. bahari*.
    2a. Sheath of No. 2.

This 'soul' (*sĕmangat*) is derived from pre-Hindu god *Sma,* whose spirit inhabits all things. *Sma* has been deposed from his godhead, first by the Hindu religion, and secondly by Islam, as he survives chiefly as a sort of clown in the *wayang kulit* (a marionette shadow show) and as this sort of soul that ancient things acquire. How it acquires this spirit it is uncertain; it is also uncertain how a *kĕris* becomes *bĕrtuwah* (lucky) possibly by age alone. It is said that a spirit was attracted to the *kĕris* during the making: that someone, usually a girl, was dedicated to it and that her spirit entered it. One story is that she was killed during the ceremony, or died when it was completed; and that her hair can be seen in the *pamor of* the blade. Another legend is that she did not die at the time of the making but was dedicated only and that at her natural death her spirit entered the blade.

In this connection may be remembered the story that the best damascus blades were tempered in the body of a slave: one man was killed to make each sword, and his spirit followed the blade. In some old weapons this *sĕmangat* may become very strong, I have told elsewhere[1] of the spear at Parit Jawa that is always kept tied up though its *sĕmangat* wishes to be free, and it is called *sĕmbilan puloh sĕmbilan* (ninety-nine) because the last time it was loose over a hundred years ago, it killed ninety-nine men; and also of a *kĕris* that is said to get thirsty for blood, to go out at night, kill someone, clean itself and come home again. Many *kĕris* are supposed to kill at a distance, merely by being pointed at the victim.

I was told by Dr. van Stein Callenfels of a raja who, having got into trouble with the Dutch authorities went with a few followers, against a whole Dutch regiment. He solemnly drew his sacred *kĕris majapahit* and pointed it, expecting to kill the entire regiment. He and his followers were all mowed down by rifle fire; but the story proves the reality of their belief in the power of the *kĕris*.

Malays say that a really powerful *kĕris,* or other weapon, should be kept tightly sheathed and always pointing upward or downward; as otherwise the evil influence will do harm and cause sickness, in the direction in which it is pointed, even though in the sheath. How much the modern Malay believes I cannot say, more than he admits I think. That older people believe in it I had proof, when a highly

---

[1] See Journal, Malayan Branch Royal Asiatic Society.

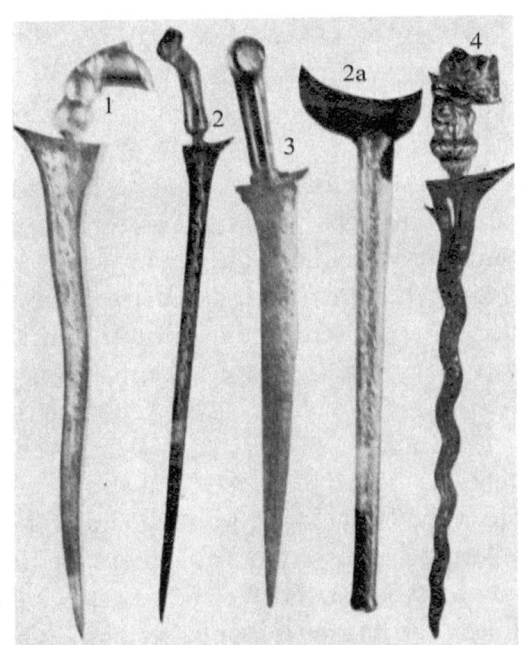

38. 1. *K. sĕmpana kĕling* with inscribed blade (also *jalar jantan*). 2. *K. bahari* with inscribed blade. 2a. Sheath of No. 2. 3. *K. jalar jantan*. 4. Balinese. *K. choban* (rusted through).

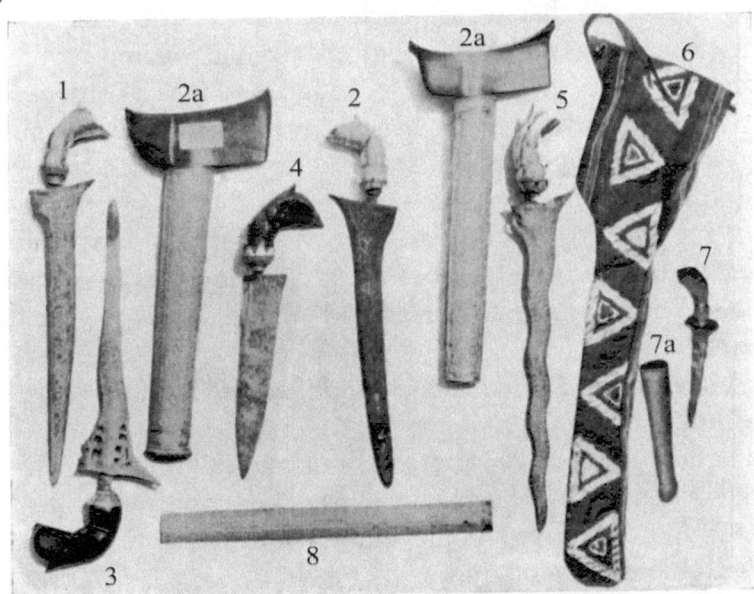

39. 1 & 1a. *K. sĕmpana* inscribed, and sheath. 2 & 2a. *K. buah beka* and sheath, (*ganja iras*). 3. *K. sĕmpana kĕling* with pierced blade also *k. naga*. 4. *K. pichit* also *k. sudu bekang*. 5. *K. bĕrpamor*. 6. Embroidered bag to protect No. 1. 7 & 7a. *K. daga* and sheath. 8. Foot rule for comparison.

educated Malay lady screamed and nearly jumped out of her chair, because a sheathed *kěris majapahit* I was showing was inadvertently pointed at her.

How the idea arose that the mere pointing of a *kěris* could kill I cannot say. Possibly some *kěris* were used as some savage tribes use pointing sticks, and the victim died of fright, or was secretly poisoned.

Malays have a much feared form of sorcery, *tuju*: pointing out a victim to a spirit of evil, or setting the spirit at him; the pointing is usually done with the finger, though I have heard of a human bone being used. Perhaps the idea of pointing the *kěris* is setting the spirit of the *kěris* (*sěmangat*) at him.

I possess a weapon, shaped like a *kěris*, but apparently of European manufacture, said to have belonged to a maharaja. It has two small pistol barrels one on each side of the blade; these are fired by triggers in the hilt. The hilt is shaped so that it must be held like a *kěris*; and by pointing and pulling the trigger it would certainly kill at a distance. (See Plate 21 No. 1).

This type of weapon may have started the stories, but I think the Malays' natural love of wonder tales had more to do with it.

Our forefathers had many such stories: the spear of Lugh for instance, if let go would fly through the air like a flame turning this way and that as the victim tried to dodge, and was so ardent that it had to be kept under water when not wanted for fear it would go killing on its own; and the hammer of Thor, which if thrown would always kill and fly back to its master's hand.

Another belief is that a man may be killed if his footprints are stabbed with a *kěris běrtuwah*. This is capable of explanation. If a *pawang* stabbed a man's footprints with a *k. běrtuwah* having taking the precaution of putting a slow poison in his rice the night before, the inference would be that he was killed by the stabbing of the footprints.

After the trick had been known to work several times, a man might well die of fright, if be heard that his footprints had been stabbed with that *kěris*. Similar power would then be attributed to other ancient *kěris*, and so the story would grow.[1]

Another queer superstition is that a certain *kěris* can draw fire; that

---

[1] c.f. the 'Angels of Mong.'

CHAPTER 1: KĚRIS

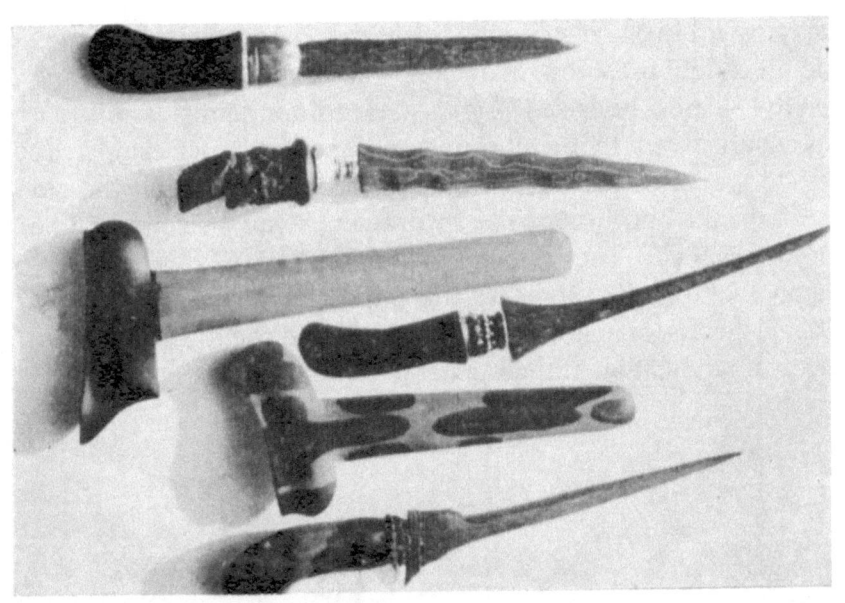

41. Javanese women's *kěris*: 6-7 ins. long.

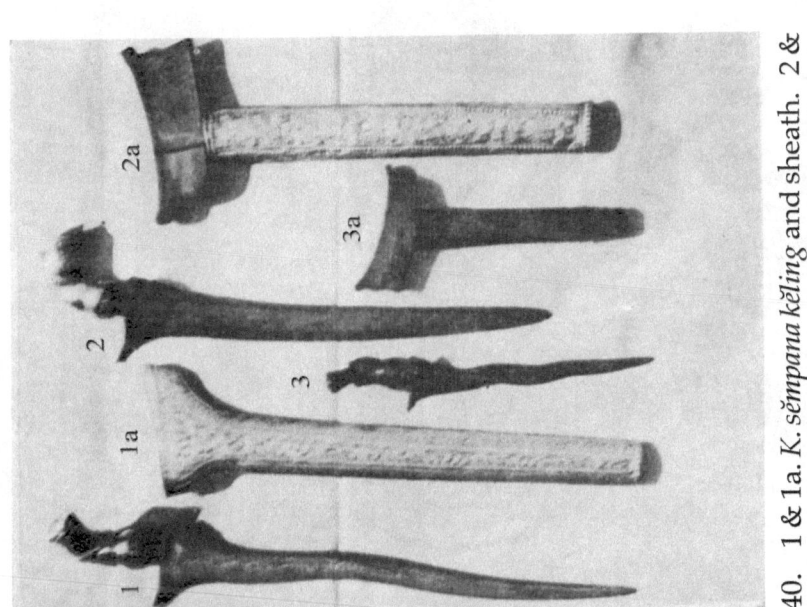

40. 1 & 1a. *K. sěmpana kěling* and sheath. 2 & 2a. Straight *kěris* (peninsular) and sheath. 3 & 3a. Very small *kěris* (northern).

is, if the house is on fire and the *kĕris* is pointed at the fire and moved to one side the fire will leave the house and follow the *kĕris*. I have an old Malay friend in Muar who only eight months ago when the next house to his caught fire, brought out a special *kĕris* and held it pointing between the burning house and his own. He triumphantly asserts that although sparks were flying all round and another house caught fire the *kĕris* stopped the fire from harming his house. I asked why he did not try to save the burning houses, by drawing away their fire, and he ingenuously replied: "They weren't my houses."

In a book of this size, however, it is impossible to describe a tenth of the *kĕris* legends, beliefs and superstitions, and the foregoing must be taken as an indication of their general trend.

42 & 43. Balinese *kĕris* holders.

IX. THE KĚRIS TO-DAY.

The *kěris* has fallen into disuse; from a sacred and royal weapon, it has become a mere curio. It was more or less inevitable. The growth of law and order would be impossible among an armed hot-tempered people, quick to resent real or imagined slights and bred with the idea that the *kěris* was the only means of settling a grievance.

Raffles says in his *History of Java*:

"The custom of wearing the *kěris* among the islanders has in its effects upon the manners of the people, proved in many respects an effectual substitute for duelling among Europeans. In these countries where there is very little justice to be obtained from the regularly established courts, and where the individual considers himself justified in taking the law into his own hands accordingly, the Malay is always prepared to avenge himself with his *kěris* the slightest insult upon the spot, but the knowledge that such an immediate appeal is always at hand prevents the necessity of its being resorted to. A habitual politeness ensues and it has been said that if the Malays are savages they are the most polite savages we know of. If this effect is produced on the wilder and less civilised Malay and has equal force with the more adventurous and warm hearted Bugis it may easily be considered the Javanese have not escaped it. The *kěris* among them has for a long period been more exclusively a personal ornament than the rapier was in Europe fifty years ago, being among the higher classes even seldomer resorted to as a weapon of defence or offence than the latter."

The same thing has happened in other countries: the Highlands had to be disarmed for the same reason; but to-day no Highland costume is complete without dirk and skeandhu and they are not misused. In Perak one often sees a Malay nobleman wearing his *kěris* as a badge of rank, and may even see it worn by a magistrate sitting on the Bench.

I hope that in future this practice may be spread, and that once again the Malay gentleman will be proud to walk abroad, wearing the *kěris*, that weapon of romance, the weapon of his ancestors.

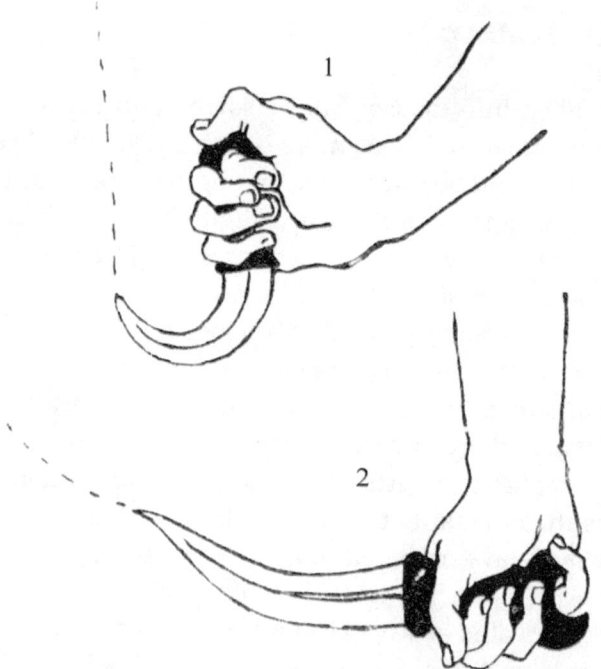

44. 1. *Lawi ayam* grip. 2. *Běladau* grip.

45. 1 & 2. Batak knife and sheath. 3. Javanese *badek*. 4. Sumatran *badek*. 5. Moluccan *pisau*.

CHAPTER 2

DAGGERS

The principal varieties of daggers are
  (1) The *jambiah*.
  (2) The *lawi ayam, kuku ayam* or *kĕrambit*.
  (3) The *bĕladau*.
  (4) The *lading tĕrus*.

(1) The *jambiah*. This is a carved dagger of Arabic or Indian origin. Native copies are also made and are found usually in Java or Sumatra: often the blade is Arabic or Indian and the hilt is made locally.

(2) The *lawi ayam* or *kuku ayam* is a small hooked knife used for ripping the bowels. It is a very horrible weapon when used on anyone with light clothing, but European clothes, especially leather belts, are some protection.

There is usually a hole in the hilt. In this the forefinger is inserted and the weapon held so that the blade projects upwards from under the little finger. It is used with an upward stroke. It can be held concealed in the hand and is essentially an assassin's weapon.

In some specimens the hole is only for ornament, being too small for use, others look. as if the upper part of the hole had been cut off leaving only the circular depression for the forefinger, but the hilt has been deliberately made this way. One explanation is that when approaching a man with a *lawi ayam* concealed in the hand the ring on the forefinger would betray its presence. It is quite possible however, that the hilt without a ring was easier to make.

I have a rare specimen where a pair fit into one sheath. The sheath is always loose, so that the weapon cannot be carried in the belt, It must be carried in the fold of the sarong or in a pocket whence it cannot fall (see Plate 44 No. 2).

A tiny variety of this weapon is said to be carried by many Javanese women, often in their hair, as a protection against rape. They are said to yield to a man, then rip his genital organ.

(3) The *Madau* is a curved single or double edged ripping dagger. Its shape is likened by Malays to be the Malayo-Arabic letter *wau*. It is like a *lawi ayam* but not so curved.

The *kěrambit* or *lawi ayam* is held as in position 1 Plate No. 44 with the forefinger through the loop, and the blade projecting under the little finger.

The *běladau* is held as in Plate 44 No. 2 with the little finger in the ring or depression. Both daggers are used with an upward ripping stroke at the stomach.

In practice the terms *lawi ayam*, *běladau* and *kěrambit* are interchangeable.

(4) The *lading těrus* is a weapon that resembles a spear blade, fitted into a dagger hilt, usually of the *lawi ayam* type, that is with a half circular depression on top of the hilt to take the little finger. The weapon, is used with an underhand thrust. I regard it as a development of the very short stabbing spear. In some places, this weapon is loosely referred to as a *běladau*.

CHAPTER 2: DAGGERS

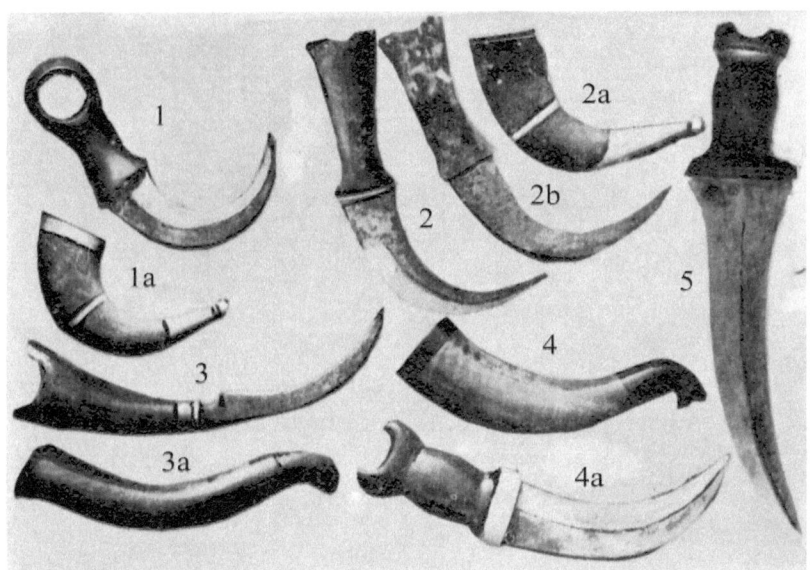

46. 1 & 1a. Lawi ayam. 2a & b. Two in one sheath: lawi ayam.
3 & 3a. Lawi ayam. 4 & 4a. Běladau. 5. Běladau.

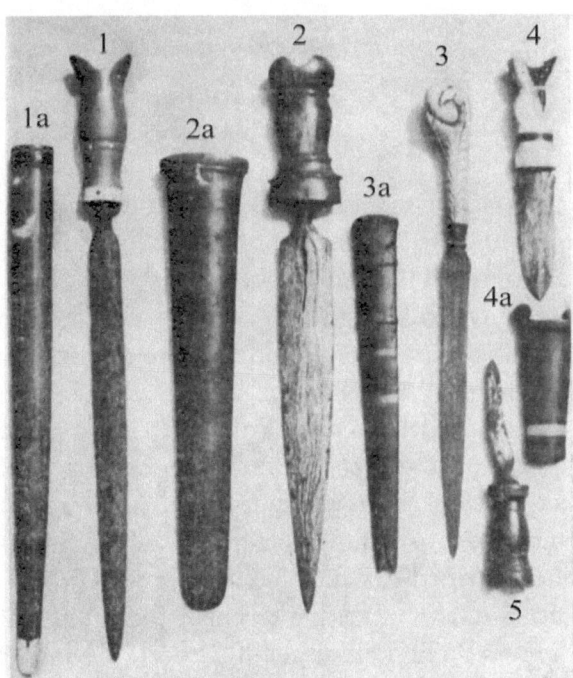

47. 1 & 1a. Lading těrus. 2. Lading těrus. 3. Lading těrus, claw hilt.
4 & 5. Lading těrus.

CHAPTER 3

SWORDS

Among Malay weapons there is a great variety of swords. The names vary very much in different localities; I have given as many as I can, but, owing to the above mentioned variation, some may appear contradictory. The same word is frequently used in different places with different meanings.

The three main types are:
   (1) The *pĕdang*.
   (2) The *golok*.
   (3) The *parang*.

(1) The *pĕdang*.

Theoretically this is any type of sword of foreign origin; but in practice the term is applied to such a sword only if it has a European type of hilt: with an Indonesian hilt it is *golok* q.v.

The *pĕdang* may be straight or curved. The straight variety is known as *chĕnangkas,* and has a blade of even width throughout. It is often sold to the unwary as a crusader's sword because the hilt is in the form of a cross with a sort of little cup for the pommel, and the purchaser is told that the crusaders used to receive the Sacramental Wine in this cup before going to battle. The smallness and lightness and poor material of the blades prove the falseness of the story and no known crusader's sword has such a hilt.

Unscrupulous dealers also try to cheat the amateur collector by selling as *chĕnangkas*, a French sergeant's sword, period about 1830, of the type called *coupe-choux*. (See Plate 48 No. 5).

The curved variety is known as *shamshir* and is a cross-hilted Indian scimitar.

CHAPTER 3: SWORDS

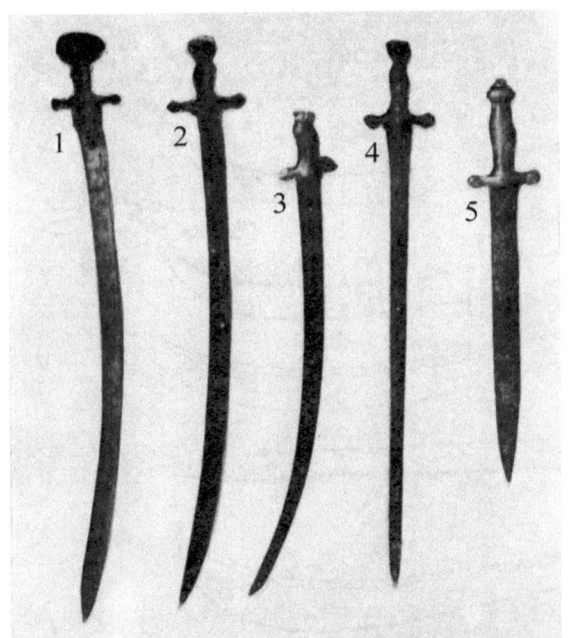

48. 1, 2 & 3. *Pĕdang shamshir,* (*tulwar*). 4. *Chĕnangkas.* 5. French sergeant's sword 1830.

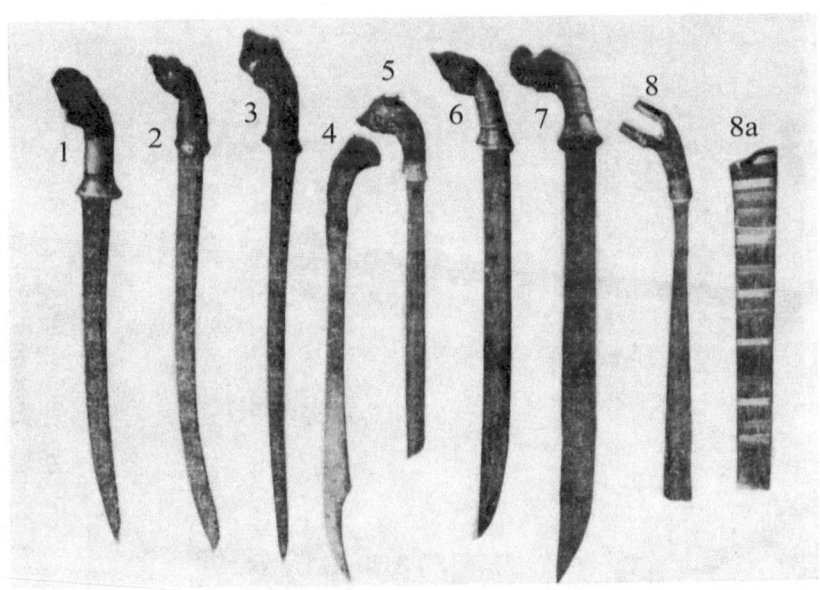

49. 1, 2 & 3. *Pĕdang bĕntok.* 4. *Kĕlewang puchok bĕrkait.* 5. *Parang.* 6 & 7. *Chundĕrik.* 8. *Lading* (Sumatran).

KERIS AND OTHER MALAY WEAPONS

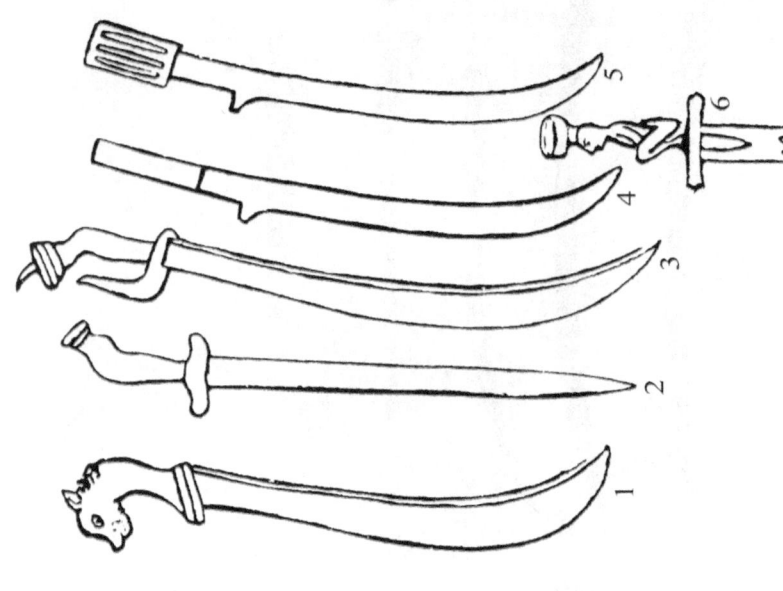

51. 1. Java: pĕdang bĕntok. 2. Java: pĕdang lurus. 3. Bali: pĕdang chĕmbul. 4. Batak: (also Acheh) pĕdang bĕntok. 5. Batak: the same with large hilt. 6. Batak: brass sword hilt, alleged Crusader type (see text).

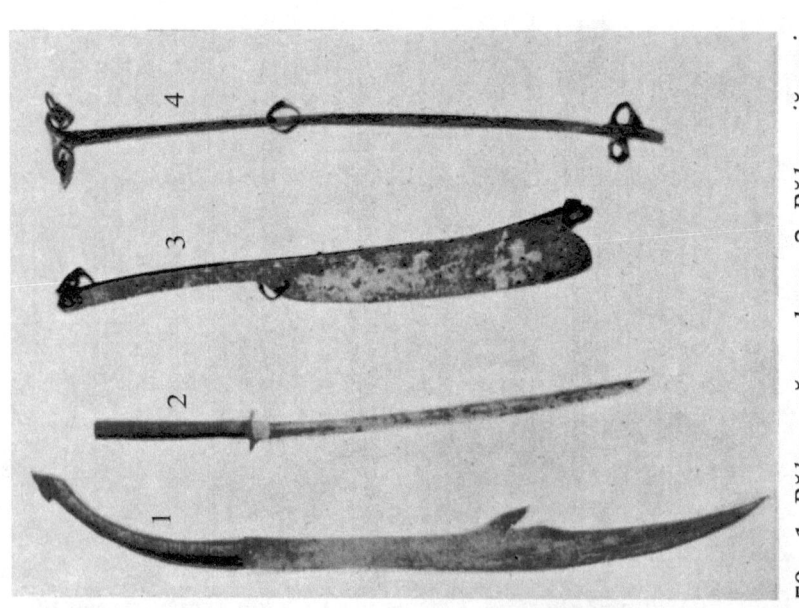

50. 1. Pĕdang pĕmanchong. 2. Pĕdang jĕnawi. 3. Parang rantai. 4. Parang rantai edgeways.

CHAPTER 3: SWORDS

These Indian swords are curved to give greater cutting power, so the boss, or pommel at the end of the hilt, is made large to prevent the sword slipping when a drawing cut is made, and it is made hollow for lightness, hence the cup shape. The two pointed lugs at the base of the handle, one on each side of the blade are typically Indian.

The type undoubtedly came from India. There is an illustration in Beveridge's *Comprehensive History of India*. Probably when the British disarmed India, quantities of Indian weapons were sold to Malaya and Java.

While many *pĕdang* seem to be of Indian workmanship, they were probably copied here also, as others are undoubtedly of Malay workmanship. The hilt is usually brass, though some are of iron or silver. I have seen one in which the hilt was of the most beautiful chased bronze (Malay work). This one had beautiful *pamor* on the blade, which is very rare. Swords of this type are often found in Sultans' regalia.

In early times, apparently, Malays used to execute by beheading, but only by the orders of the ruler. This can be deduced from the various sayings: *kĕris pĕnggalan daripada undang, pĕdang pĕmanchong daripada kĕadilan* ('a *kĕris* that executes bloodlessly comes from the chief, but the sword that beheads from the ruler.' Nĕgĕri Sembilan saying) and *pĕdang pĕmanchong raja yang ĕmpunya* ('the execution sword belongs to the ruler').

I have not been able to find out what the *pĕdang pĕmanchon* was really like though I have one so called (see Plate 50 No. 1). It is very heavy and wonderfully balanced and would do the work splendidly. The hilt, which is of brass inlaid with a kind of lac (*ĕmbalau*) is in dragon form and looks like Siamese work: but as I am told a sword like that has never been used in Siam, it may be Malay. The man from whom I got it told me that in ancient times it was used in the Northern states under Siamese rule in a form of execution by torture: a victim was hung by the legs from two posts and split down the centre till half hung to each post. I have not yet been able to verify this and give it for what it is worth. I mentioned it because I cannot find any trace of another execution sword. Another name for it is *pĕdang mĕngerat leher-leher*.

Pĕdang jĕnawi. This is a long two handed sword from the far east. Chinese or Japanese swords are of this type and may be straight or

KERIS AND OTHER MALAY WEAPONS

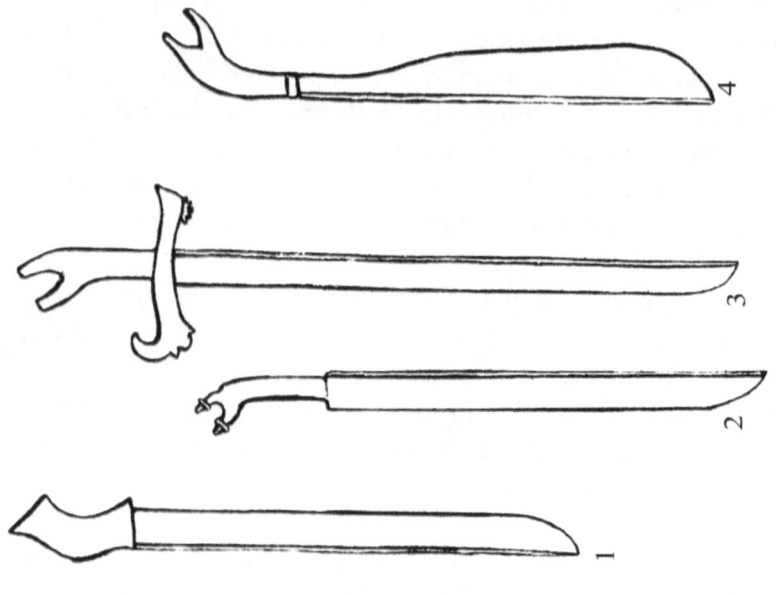

52. 1. Java: *sikim*. 2. Batak and Acheh: *sikim*. 3. Acheh: *sikim*. 4. Acheh: *sikim gajah*.

53. 1. *Parang jengkok*. 2. Kělantan: *parang bengkok*. 3. *Golok jambu*. 4 & 5. Java: *kudik*.

curved (see Plate 50 No. 2). This specimen was dug up in Muar and fitted with a wooden handle.

A beautiful specimen of *pĕdang jĕnawi*, hilt and sheath covered with Malay gold work, is with the Riau regalia in the Batavia Museum.

Pĕdang jĕnawi are of far eastern, possibly Japanese origin. Both the Portuguese and the Dutch employed Japanese as mercenaries and they left many of their weapons behind them. These were undoubtedly used by the Malays, being of very fine steel.

Other varieties of *pĕdang* are:
    p. bĕrtupai: Indian tulwar, a basket hilted sword.
    p. chĕmbul: also a basket hilted sword.
    p. rajawali: swords in Perak regalia.
    p. pĕrbayangan:
    p. bĕntok: swords with curved blades.
    p. chakok:
    p. bĕrandal: a heavy Borneo type of sword.

(2) The *golok*.

The *golok* is a sword with a convex cutting edge. The term *golok* is applied to Javanese swords or European curved sabre blades with Indonesian hilts: with European hilts they are also called *sikim*; but the term *sikim* should, theoretically, be restricted to straight one-edged sword blades of even width, of native make. In Acheh *sikim* is applied to all swords of the *golok* type.

Varieties of the *golok* are:
Golok jambu or the Kĕlantan *kĕlewang*. This is short and curved (see Plate 53 No. 3). It has a sharp spike at the back. The bearer of this weapon will it is said, pass his enemy with the *golok jambu* swinging idly in his hand. The enemy will watch carefully until he imagines the danger is past; then without turning the bearer will swing the *golok jambu* up over his shoulder when the spike pierces his enemy's brain.

The late Mr. Cyril Blair Cooper told me that a similar trick was much used in Johore when he first settled there. However, the Johore Malays used ordinary *parang* tied to a whippy *rotan*.

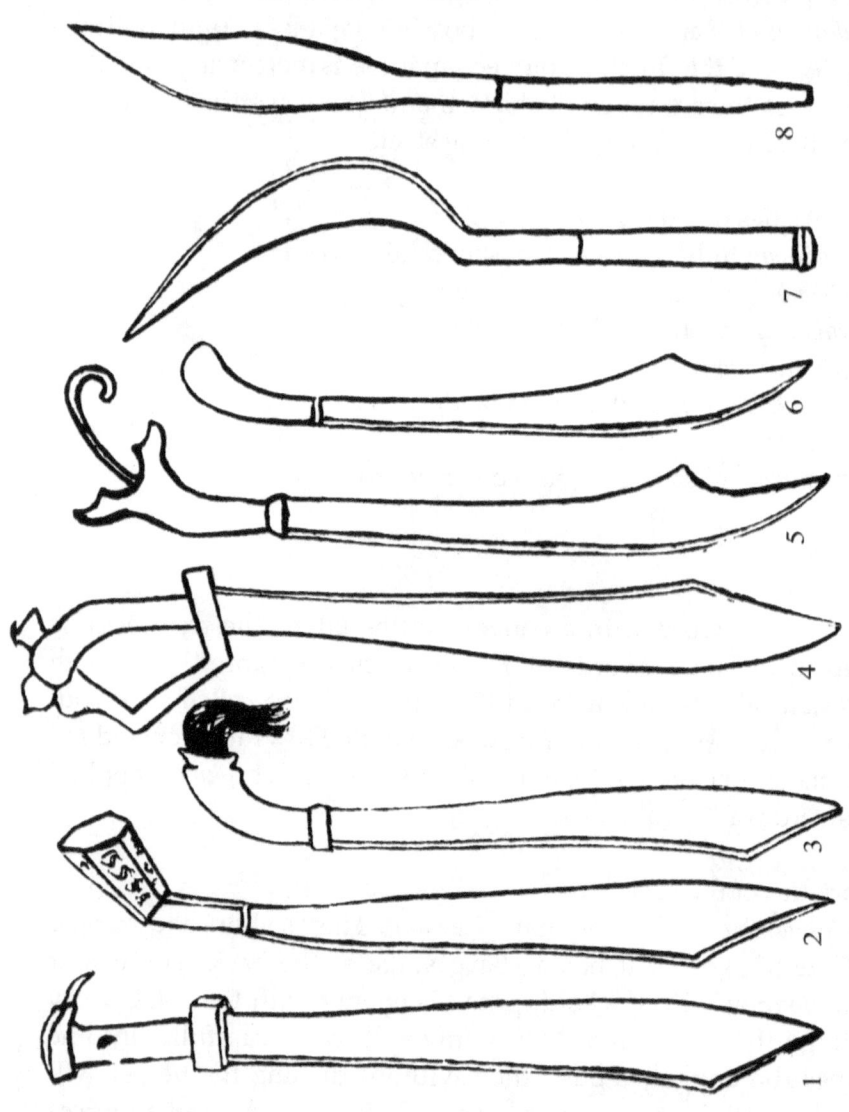

54. 1, 2, 3, 4. *Kĕlewang*. 5. W. Sumatra: *kĕlewang puchok bĕrkait*. 6. Acheh: the same. 7 & 8. Bali: *arit*.

CHAPTER 3: SWORDS

The *sulu kĕlewang*. A single edge sword that gets wider and heavier towards the point. The cutting edge is straight. This is what used to be called in Europe a hand and a half, or bastard sword. The hilt being made so that it can be used single or double handed, it is often made with a spike on the slope of the blade.

The *gĕdubang* is a sword of the *kĕlewang* type, short and heavy.

The *ilanun kampilan* is the longest variety of the *golok* and the *gĕdubang* the shortest.

The *kĕlewang tĕbal hujong* thickens as well as broadens towards the point. The *kĕlewang puchok bĕrkait* has a curving point.

The *golok bangkong* or *golok pĕrak* broadens towards the centre. The *tarah baju* is the Achehnese equivalent of the *golok*.

The *bĕladau* (not to be confused with the dagger of that name) is a heavy *golok* or leaf shaped sword used by the Bajaus in Borneo and also in Sulu. It has a characteristic hilt (see Plate 86 No. 1). It is a terrible weapon at close quarters, especially in a house, where the longer weapons would be impeded in use. The term is sometimes used to describe a short Turkish type of sword.

(3) The *parang*.

The *parang* is a kind of cleaver. The special feature of the *parang* is that the cutting edge is usually convex, and the blade gets broader and heavier as it leaves the handle.

Varieties of the *parang* are:

P. rantai, or *chĕriga*. This is a *parang* with an iron hilt. At the slope, the hilt and the bottom of the blade there are projecting spirals made of the metal of the blade, to which are attached chains.

It was said to be talismanic, to effect a cure if placed beneath a sick person's bed, and was laid on the bodies of the dead.

I have only seen two specimens. I showed these to several old people on the Johore River. They recognised them as *p. rantai* and said that they were very old and *bĕrtuwah*. They told me however, that the mode of use and the powers that *p. rantai* were supposed to have had, were forgotten. There is a fine specimen in the Batavia Museum. The only information available was that it came from the Celebes and probably had magical powers. It was called 'tjoeriga.'

KERIS AND OTHER MALAY WEAPONS

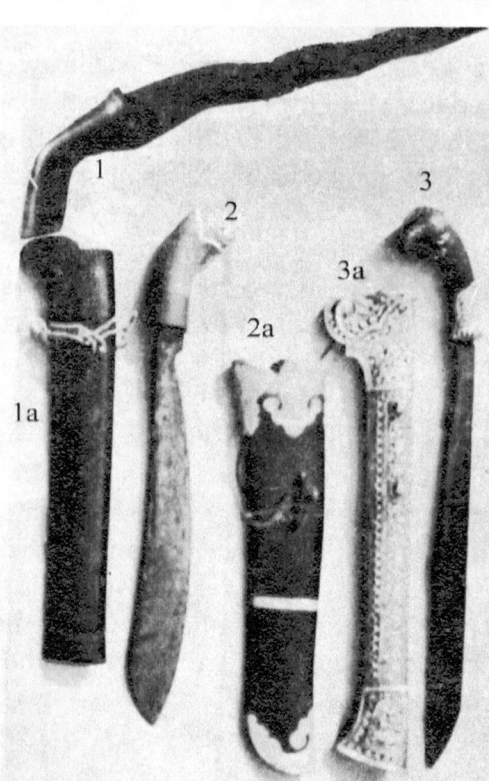

55. 1 & 1a. *Parang sari* and *sheath*.
2 & 2a. *Parang* and *sheath*.
3 & 3a. *Parang* and silver sheath.

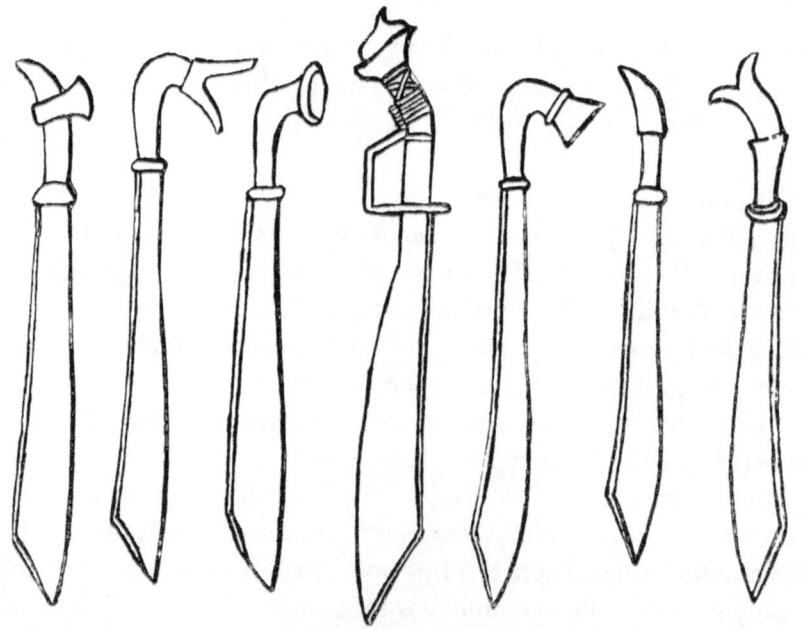

56. Celebes: *kĕlewang*.

CHAPTER 3: SWORDS

P. sari.[1] I have a weapon called *parang sari,* the only one of its kind I have ever seen. It feels like a cutting weapon and has a *parang* hilt, but the blade is waved like a *kĕris* and has a partly blunt edge (*mampai*). (See Plate 55 No. 1). It is a combination weapon and jungle knife. The Malay wearing this apparently harmless *parang* (a small *parang* would wound but not kill) could come to close quarters with an unsuspecting enemy, then draw suddenly, when the victim would be at his mercy.

The *parang sari* is mentioned in old romances: *ada parang sari sa-bĕlah tujoh-bĕlas lok-nya*: 'there was once a *parang sari* with seventeen waves in the blade.'

Other varieties are:
- *p. panggong* long and sword-like.
- *p. lading*
- *p. bangkong*
- *p. pandak* short and heavy not markedly concave.
- *p. gondok*
- *p. lotok* short and heavy with a hooked point also called *p. Patani.*
- *p. chakok* a bill hook.
- *p. bengkok*
- *p. ongkok* } all markedly concave.
- *p. pajah*
- *p. koteng* having hilt and blade in one piece.
- *p. chandong*
- *p. pĕranggi* handle and blade in one piece.
- *p. gabus* highly tempered.
- *p. sa-kampok* tempered and much sharpened; used in the jungle as a weapon also.

Barong is the name by which *parang* are known in the Philippines.

---

[1] This weapon is sometimes confused with *kĕris parong sari* (q.v.) because Wilkinson in the first edition of his Dictionary so confuses them; in the second edition, however, he recognises that *parang* and *parong*, though similar in sound, are of different derivation. (BLM)

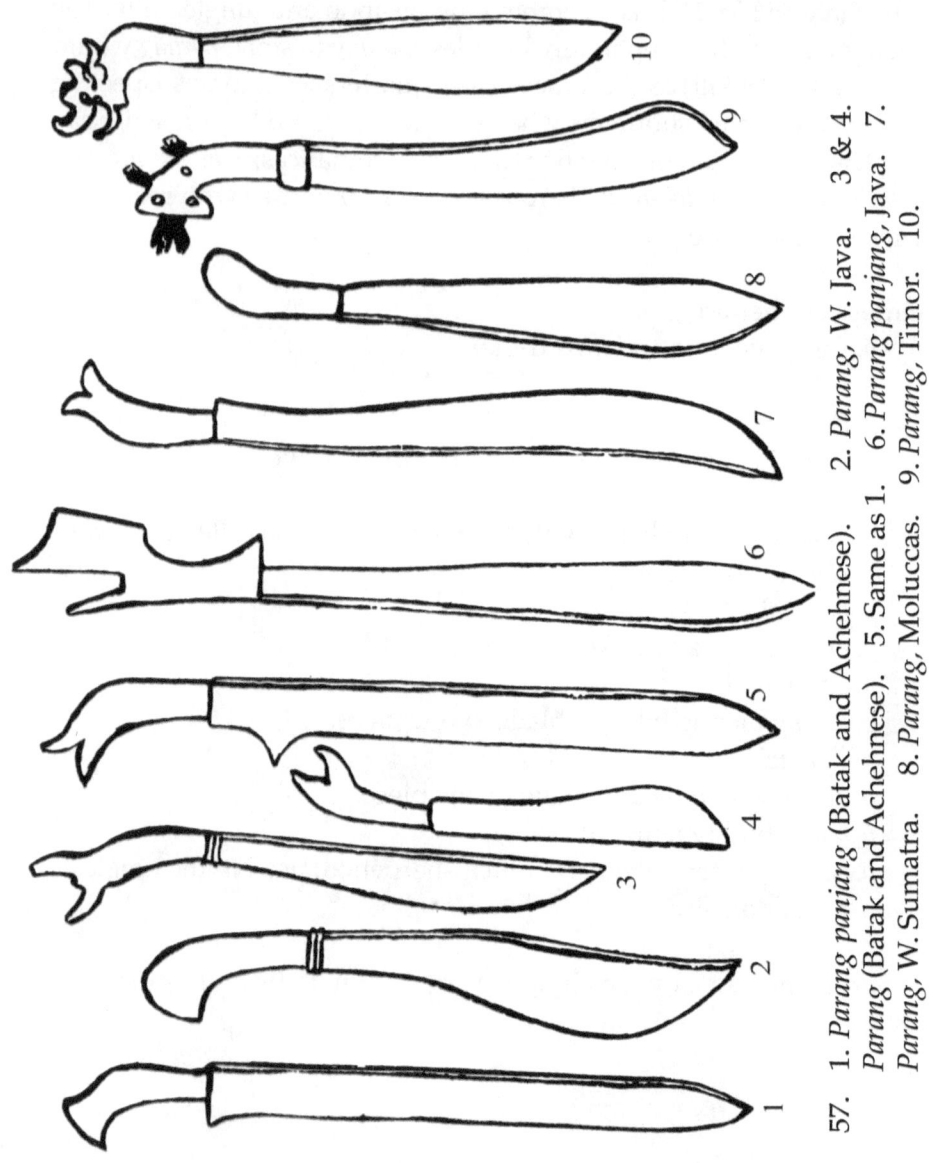

57. 1. *Parang panjang* (Batak and Achehnese). 2. *Parang*, W. Java. 3 & 4. *Parang* (Batak and Achehnese). 5. Same as 1. 6. *Parang panjang*, Java. 7. *Parang*, W. Sumatra. 8. *Parang*, Moluccas. 9. *Parang*, Timor. 10.

VARIOUS

Baur a sword of office, given to each of a number of Perak dignitaries on his installation and returned at his death. After the Perak War, these were sent to Singapore and some were lost altogether.

Chundĕrik (the Javanese *kudi*) in various forms: sometimes a knife, sometimes a long handled chopper, sometimes hafted as a spear. The former are occasionally too small to be of any use. It was talismanic in the days when iron was scarce, and was often carried by a *pawang* (magician) as a symbol of his craft. Under another name, *chura si-manjakini*, it is a dynastic sword of Malay Sultans.

Wedung is a type of *parang* worn by chiefs in Java, having a long horn spur to slip into the belt. On state occasions these chiefs may only wear one *kĕris* and that at the back; and the wearing of the *wedung* is intended to symbolise their readiness to cut down *bĕlukar* (undergrowth) or do anything else their sovereign may require. (See Plate 61).

KERIS AND OTHER MALAY WEAPONS

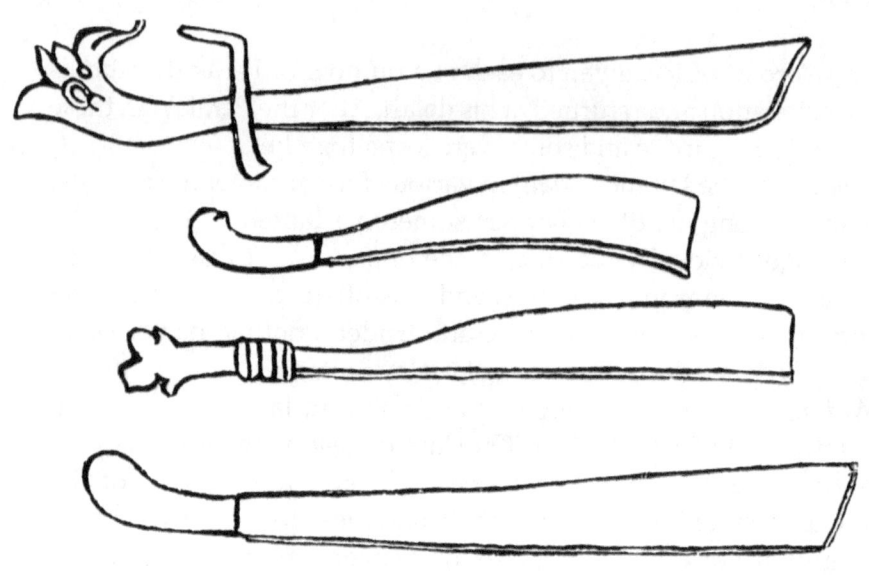

59. *Parang lading.*

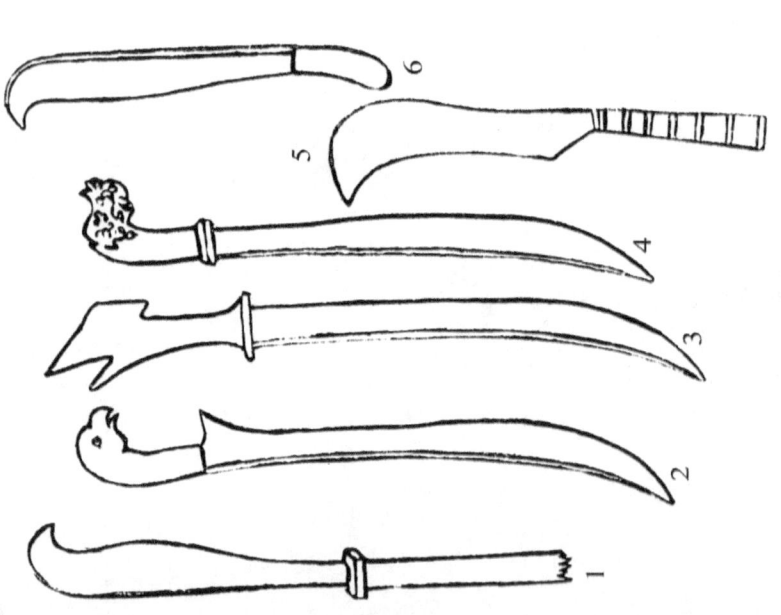

58. 1. *Parang bengkok* (Bali). 2. *Pĕdang bĕntok or golok* (Bali). 3. *Mang bĕntok or golok* (Java). 4. Same as 2. 5 & 6. *Parang bengkok* (Java).

CHAPTER 3: SWORDS

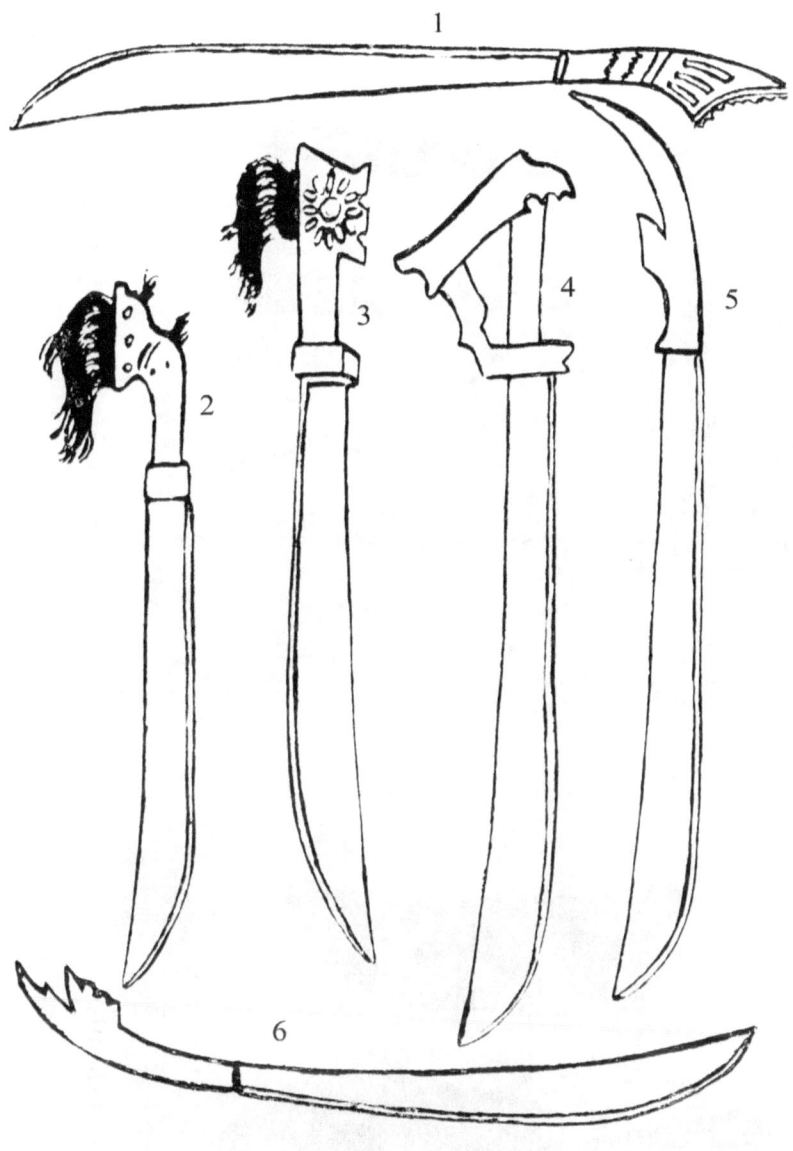

60. *Chunděrik*. 1. W. Sumatra. 2. Moluccas. 3 & 4. Timor. 5. Java. 6. Acheh.

KERIS AND OTHER MALAY WEAPONS

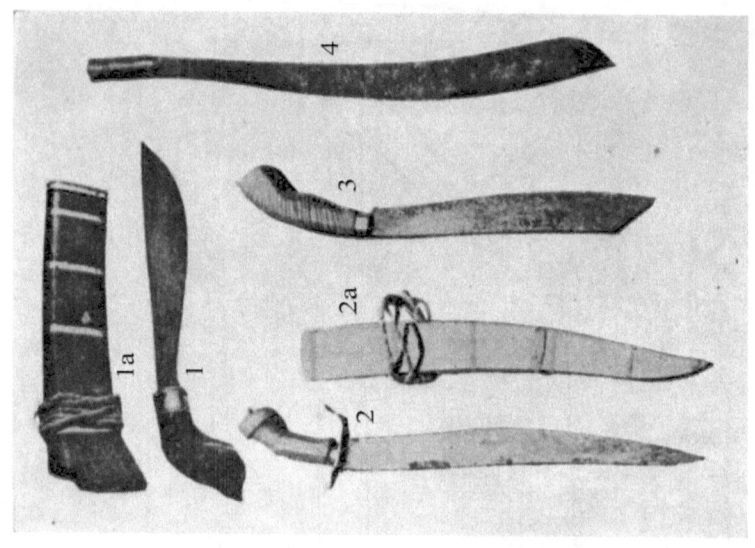

62. 1 & 1a. Malay *parang* and *sheath*. 2 & 2a. Philippine *parang* and sheath (*barong*). 3. Philippine tool. 4. Malay *parang* with iron handle.

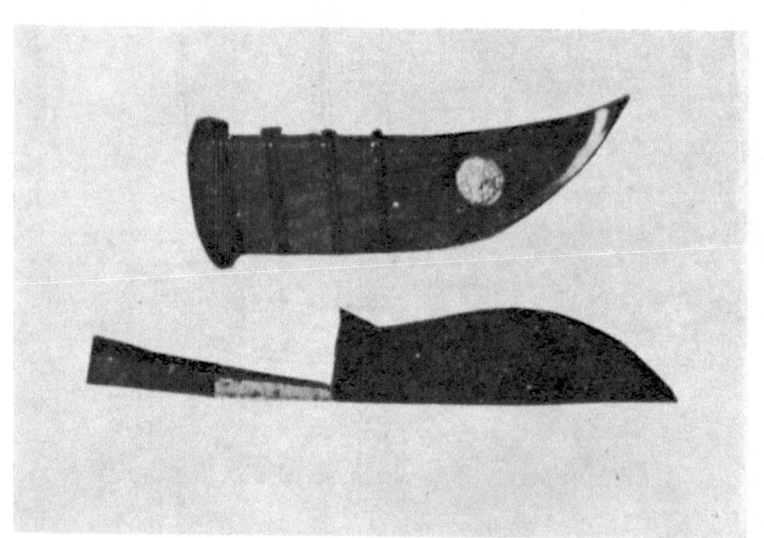

61. *Wedung* and sheath.

CHAPTER 3: SWORDS

63. Timor *kĕlewang*

CHAPTER 4

SPEARS

Malays used many spears and javelins. The general name for spears is *tombak*.

(1) THRUSTING SPEARS.
These spears seldom if ever have a socket. The head has a long tang which is fitted into the shaft and fastened with resin. The shaft is fitted with a long ferrule (*těmin*) usually of brass or silver to prevent splitting. The silver ones are often beautifully worked. In Borneo a spearhead is lashed on with rotan and sometimes with brass wire.

Lěmbing. This is a specific name for spears with a ridge down the centre of the blade. These are characteristic of the Peninsula. They seem to have been modelled on the old Chinese bronze age spears. This ridge pattern is certainly an old type. Plate 80 shows an iron *lěmbing*, a bronze *lěmbing* and a broken stone spearhead all with a ridge. It should be remembered that bronze weapons were not in use in Malaya until a short time ago, and that the later polished stone weapons were copies of the bronze or iron ones. The early stone spearheads did not show this ridge (see Plate 80 No. 2) because they were not copied from bronze or iron weapons.

sěrunjong:	This is a sharpened stake or spike used as a spear or pike, not used for throwing.
chandak	is a short stabbing spear, similar to an assegai.
sodok	a broad-bladed spear-like weapon.
ranggas	a lance used for tilting in tournaments.
kujur	a fish spear or a heavy pike.

CHAPTER 4: SPEARS

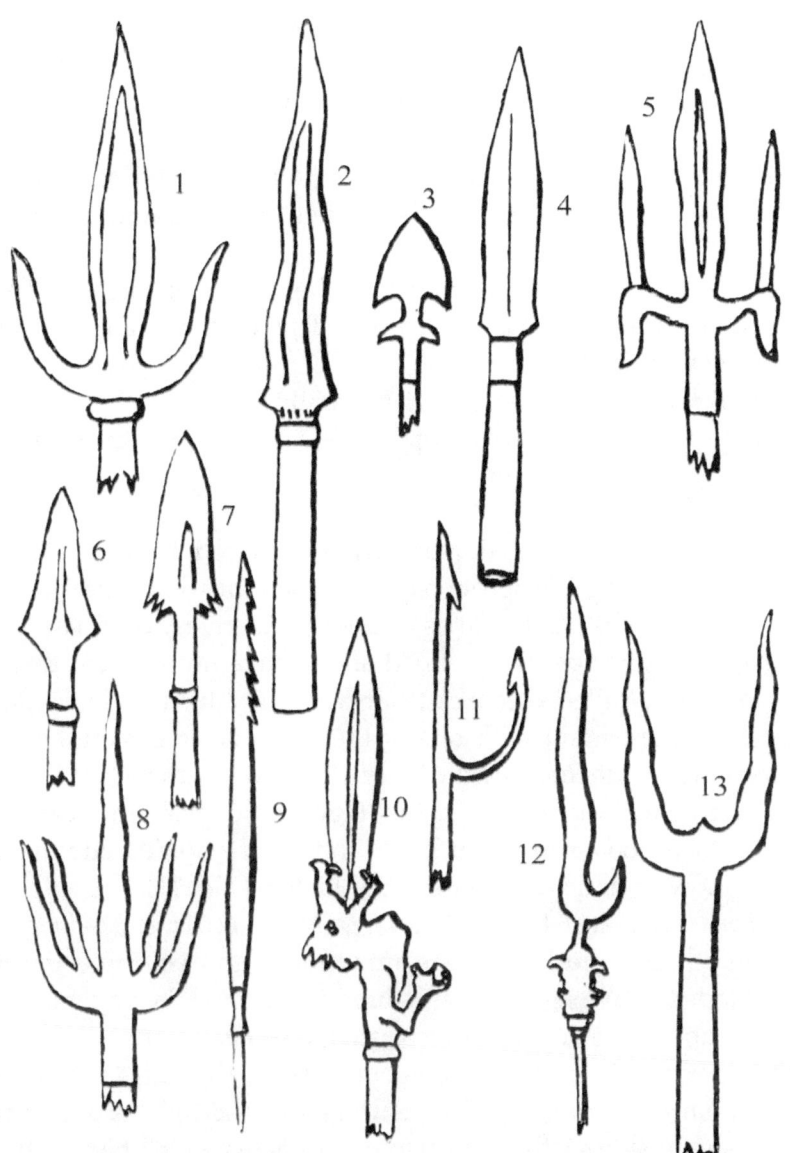

64. 1 & 5. *Těrisula* or *běsi tiga* (Java).   2. Short handled stabbing spear (Bali).   3. *Lěmbing* (Batak).   4. As 2 (Java).   6 & 7. *Lěmbing* (W. Sumatra).   8. *Lěmbing, běsi lima* (Java).   9, 10 & 12. *Lěmbing* (Java). 11. *Tipu Dayak* (Malaya).   13. *Lěmbing, běsi dua* (Bali).

Note: These spear heads are not all on the same scale.

tombak pěngawinan   a halberd. In the Peninsula it is only found in the Malacca district and is of Portuguese, Dutch or Japanese origin, or is a native copy of these.

tombak běnděrang   a spear of state. Four or seven of these are carried before chiefs in procession.

The shaft is ornamented with hair or horse tails or yak tails. These are dyed crimson or crimson and white. This type may also be called *tombak rambu* (tufted spear).

Tombak kěrajaan   state spears generally.

Galaganjar.   This is a pike used as an emblem of rank in Riau.

Gěganit. This is a corruption of the English word 'bayonet.' Malays often mount European bayonets on poles and use them as spears. On old battlefields I have dug up many of these.

Tipu Dyak. The spears described above have no barb but there is a variety called *tipu dyak* (to trick the Dyak). This looks like a Neptune trident with one of the side blades cut off, and the central blade made a little longer. The story is that Dyaks would charge with such violence that they would receive a spear point in their body, run up the blade and kill the holder; and the *tipu dyak* was made to stop this. (See Plate 64 No. 11).

Běsi dua (see Plate 64 No. 13), *běsi tiga* (Nos. 1 & 5) and *běsi lima* (No. 8). In Java and Bali spears are found with two, three and five blades. I have seen one with three blades but this is a ceremonial weapon. The *běsi tiga* is also called *těrisula*.

Sěrampang. This is a trident weapon used by the Bugis both in war and for spearing fish. The central spike had two barbs and was usually shorter than the two outer spikes which had barbs on the inner side only (see Plate 65 No. 1).

Torak. This is a fishing trident only: unlike the *sěrampang* the *torak* is loose and the shaft comes away.

There is also a very short stabbing spear for which I can get no name, it appears to be an ordinary spear with a shaft cut short to a length of one foot; but, from there being several specimens in the various Sultans' regalia in the Batavia Museum I think they may be

CHAPTER 4: SPEARS

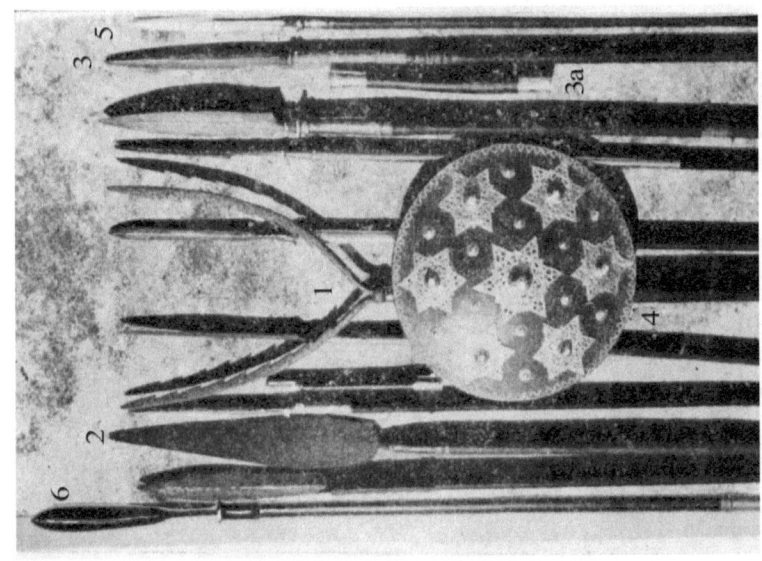

66. 1. *Sangga mara.* 2. Large spear from Kĕlantan. 3 & 3a. Malay spear with central ridge and sheath. 4. Shield. 5. Bronze walking spear. 6. Short stabbing spear.

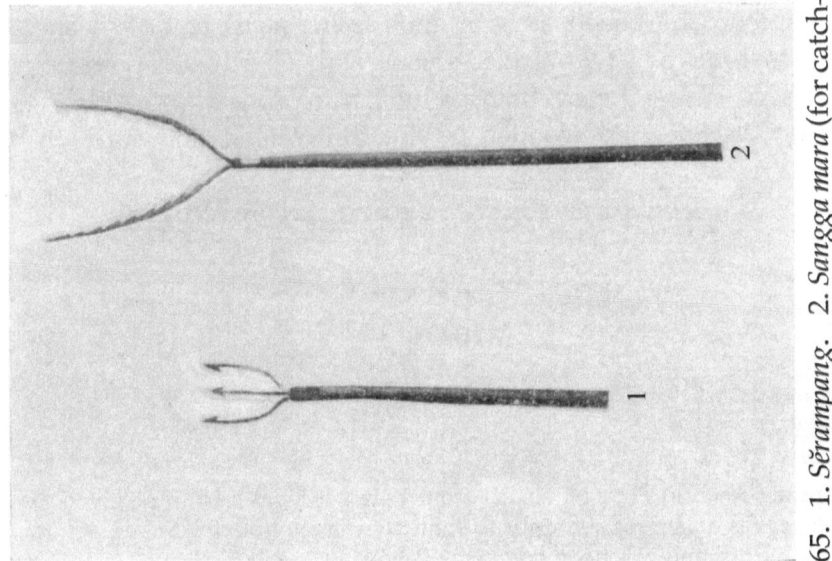

65. 1. *Sĕrampang.* 2. *Sangga mara* (for catching *amok*).

classed as a distinct weapon, probably the origin of the dagger called *lading těrus*, q.v.

The Javanese made a ceremonial spear in the form of a grotesque animal, with a big protruding tongue which formed the spear blade (see Plate 64 No. 10).

The following expressions in connection with spears may be of interest.

Main tombak di-alas kuda: A Javanese tournament between lance or spear armed horsemen.

Tujah: stabbing downwards: e.g. through a lath floor at a man spying under a Malay house.

Radak: stabbing upwards; e.g. through the lath floor at a man sleeping in a Malay house.

Tikam tandang: execution with the javelin; hurling a spear at a fleeing man and so degrading him to the position of a hunted animal.

(2) THROWING SPEARS.

Pěndahan a javelin or dart held by the hand.

Sěligi wooden dart or javelin. This is sometimes a light strip of bamboo sharpened at both ends (*sěligi tajam běrtimbal*) and sometimes a heavy wooden javelin with a hardwood point.

Sagu sagu	a javelin used by Ilanun pirates.
Champak buang	a wooden javelin thrown but not worth retrieving.
Tohok	a javelin with a rope to secure recovery.

Note:
[1] The spear shown in Plate 66 No. 21 from Kělantan, was said to be given to messengers as a mark of authority, to show they came from the Sultan. It had no central ridge and was not made in the Peninsula.
[2] There is also in Raffles Museum a barbed, single-bladed spear called *běndera*. The word means 'Flag,' and the spear has the appearance of a flag hanging from *a* pole: alternatively, it may be compared to a *tipu dyak* without the 2nd blade.

CHAPTER 4: SPEARS

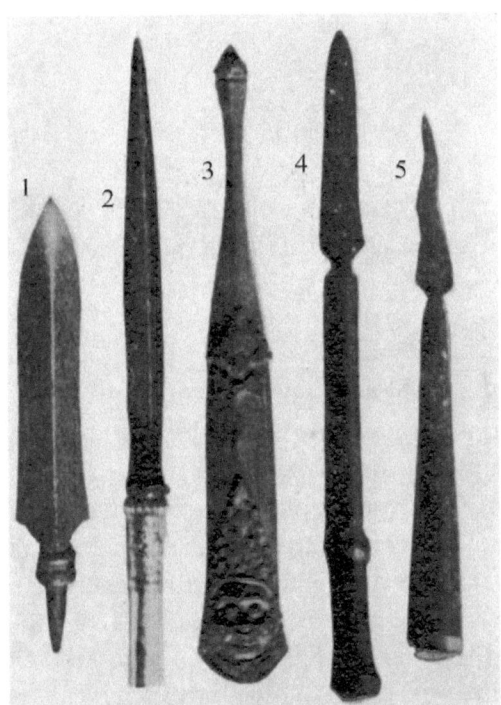

67. 1 & 2. *Lĕmbing*. 3. Spear sheath. 4 & 5. *Chandak,* stabbing spear.

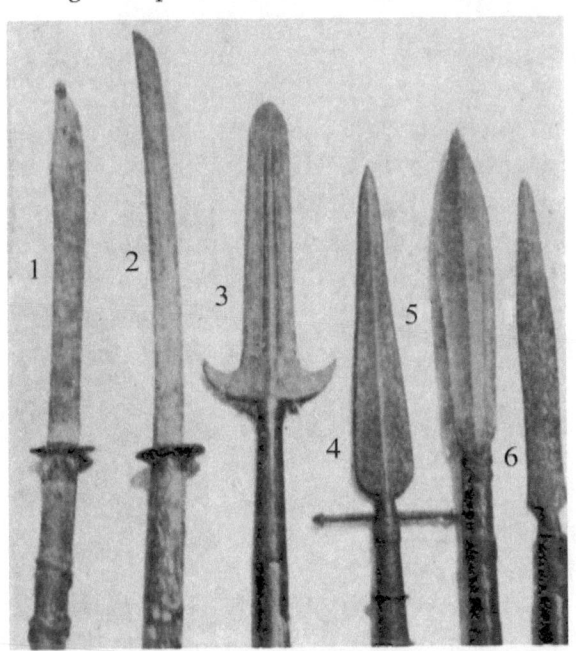

68. 1 & 2. *Tombak pĕngawinan*. 3. *Tombak pĕngawinan* probably from Ceylon. 4. *Tombak pĕngawinan* (Dutch). 5 & 6. Borneo spears.

CHAPTER 5

CANNON

The Malays used to make cannon in Trěngganu, Java, Měnangkabau, Acheh, on the Johore River and probably in other places.

Marsden, in his *History of Sumatra* (1811) says:

"We meet with accounts in old writers of great foundries of cannon in Acheh and it is certain that firearms as well as *kěris* are at this time manufactured in the country of Měnangkabau. Their guns are matchlocks. The improvement of springs and flints not being adopted by them, the barrels are well tempered and of the justest bore, their aim is excellent, which they take by lowering the muzzle at the object. They are made by rolling a bar of flatted iron round a circular rod, the art of boring[1] is probably unknown to them. Gunpowder they make in great quantities but it is very poor."

He goes on to say that gunpowder was manufactured in various parts of the, island. It was made, as with us, with proportions of charcoal, sulphur and nitre; but the composition was very imperfectly graduated, being often hastily prepared in small quantities for immediate use. Nitre was found in saltpetre caves, but for the most part was procured from goats' dung, which was always to be had in plenty. Sulphur (*bělerang*) is procured from volcanos.

The following are the usual types:
   (1) *Měriam*
   (2) *Lela*
   (3) *Rěntaka*
   (4) *Ekur lotong*

---

[1] In Lombok, guns were made by boring iron bars.

CHAPTER 5: CANNON

69. *Měriam.*

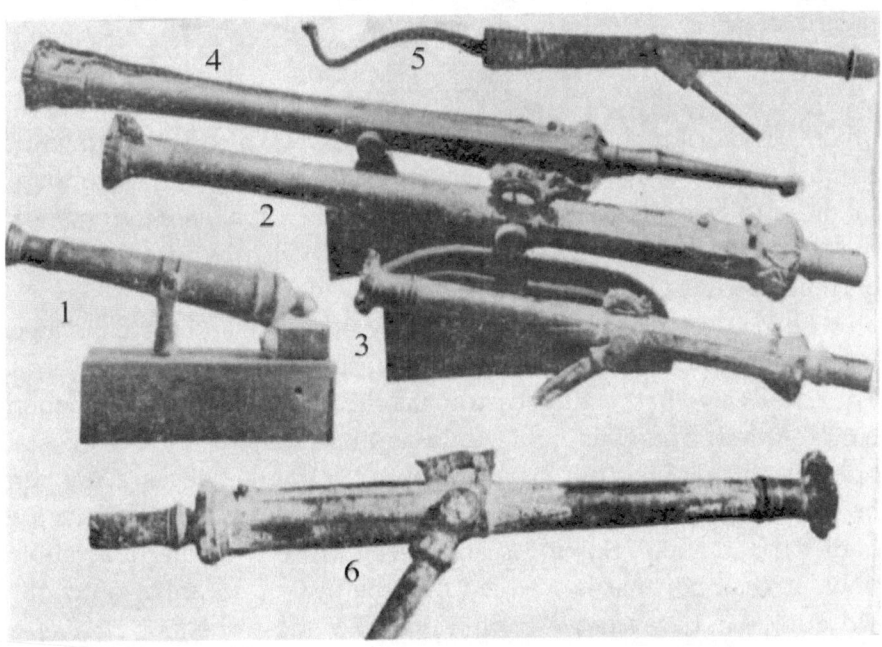

70. 1. *Měriam kalok.* 2 & 3. *Lela.* 4. *Lela rambang* (note wooden peg).
    5. *Ekur lotong.* 6. *Lela* (note dolphins on Nos 2, 3 & 6).

(1) *Měriam*: The name is the equivalent of 'Mary'; probably an early gun was so named. It carries a ball of six pounds or more. It is probably a copy of the European demiculverin. It is often highly ornamented and usually has the dolphins, the twin lugs on the top of the gun just above the trunnions, for hoisting the gun on board ship. These are often made in the form of dolphins, as in the best Spanish and Dutch models. (See Plate 69).

Subdivisions of these types are:
(a) *Měriam agong*, heavy and double barrelled.
(b)   "   *buloh*, long smooth and cylindrical.
(c)   "   *jolong* or *jěnjulong*, long tapering and narrow calibred.
(d)   "   *kalok*, short and squat.
(e)   "   *dua sa-kalam*, bow guns in pairs.
(f)   "   *pěminggang*, central battery guns.
(g)   "   *turat* sternchasers.

In Java the *měriam* type is called *bědil*. The subdivisions are:
(a) *Bědil běsar*   heavy guns, especially of very old types.
(b)   "   *pěngatu*, obsolete.
(c)   "   *těgadas*, obsolete.

(2) *Lela*: The original gun of this type was cast by a coppersmith after a model supplied by a Captain Lucas (*sěri lukas*) to Sultan Ala'udin of Johore, and was named after the heroine of the *Laila Majnun* romance; the name was then given to long barrelled swivel guns generally. Short barrelled swivel guns were called *tomong*.

The *lela* was made of brass, or more rarely iron, and corresponded to the European falcon or falconet. Its ordinary range was 400 yards. The *lela* always had a tube cast in the breach, into which a wooden handle fitted. This was held while aiming and firing the gun. *Lela* often have dolphins but they are purely ornamental; as a *lela* can be picked up there is no need to hoist it. Those made in Brunei are highly ornamented. Some *lela* are breech loaders, having a separate powder chamber that is wedged into the breech. In imitation of the old European base *lela* were often placed at the corners of stockades so as to fire down two faces. They are also much used on the rails of boats. Some *lela* are double barrelled. All *lela* and other swivel guns

CHAPTER 5: CANNON

71. *Leta rambang.*

72. *Rĕntaka.*

have a forked mount (*changkak tela* or *rangking*) with a long spike that fits into the rail of a boat, or the edge of a stockade. Although these guns are now usually seen mounted on small carriages, the latter are for show purposes only, since the advantage of the *lela* was that it could be fixed in places where there was no room for a gun carriage. Moreover, being a swivel it could be easily turned in any direction without the necessity of turning the carriage.

Some *lela* have a bore of only ¾ inch, I suppose the shortage of small arms was the reason for the making of these. Malays also made numbers of tiny cannon, with bores of ½ inch to 1 inch. These were mostly toys, but I believe in war a number were sometimes used to defend a gateway. A row fastened to a log and charged with slugs would cause damage at close range. I have seen three barrelled specimens that were obviously made for this purpose. Also in Brunei, some big *lela* had one or more of these little guns cast on the top of their barrels for use if the enemy charged before the *lela* could be reloaded.

The *lela rambang* was a brass *lela* with a blunderbuss muzzle which fired slugs or stones; corresponding to the European cannon perrier, or murdering pieces, which were murder at short range. It is also sometimes called *lela mulut katak* (the frog-mouthed gun) (see Plate 71).

(3) The *rintaka*, an iron cannon. Malays say they used to make them but all I have seen seem to be of European manufacture.

(4) The *ekur lotong*: These were sometimes made by Malays, of iron forged round a mandrel. They have a curved iron handle forged on, resembling the tail of a *lotong* monkey. They are copies of European swivel guns carried on ship's rails.

In the old battlefields on the Johore River there are found stone balls up to 8 ½ inches in diameter. These would fit the double cannon, or cannon royal, of the time of Charles I and Charles II. I think these guns must have been imported, but as none of them have been found yet, it is impossible to be sure. However as the ball are found at times in the walls of old forts, there is no doubt that they were used.[1]

---

[1] These balls may have been fired from the guns of a European attacking force. (BLM)

CHAPTER 5: CANNON

73. Miniature cannon. Note the weapon in the form of a bull, which fires through the rear orifice, a symbol of humorous contempt.

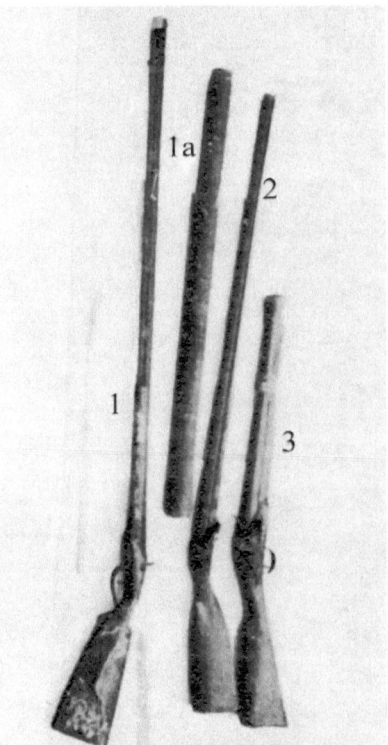

74. 1. Long flintlock gun ornamented.   1a. Bamboo and *rotan* case.
    2. Flintlock gun.   3. Brass blunderbuss.

Nearly all Malay guns would seem to have been fired with a lintstock (slow match in the holder). This was called *tali api* and was usually a piece of coconut husk. There is one in Taiping that has been cast so as to take a flintlock, though this is now missing. Malay cannon usually fired stone balls, though iron ones were also used, and a brass ball has been found. They used lead and tin slugs at close quarters, and made a sort of case shot of stones in a *rotan* basket.

CHAPTER 6

SMALL ARMS

The general term for guns, muskets and rifles is *sĕnapang*. Varieties of *sĕnapang* are:
(1) *sĕnapang batu*: flintlock.
(2) *s. kĕmbar* (or *pĕngantin*) double barrelled.
(3) *s. pĕrdiul* muzzle loading cap gun.
(4) *s. kĕpok* magazine rifle.
(5) *s. kulai* (or *patok*) breech loader.
(6) *s. tĕrkul* rifle.
(7) *s. pukol* the old muzzle loader, the ball of which had to be hammered down the barrel with a mallet.
(8) *s. bĕdil pĕmuras* blunderbuss. Another name for this is *mulut bĕrkĕchubong* (bell-mouthed).
(9) *bĕdil istinggar*, matchlock (probably from the Portuguese *espingarda*).

Most Malay smalls arms, and all flintlocks, seem to have been imported. They made gun barrels, however, by wielding bar iron round a mandrel and occasionally by boring out an iron bar. The locks of *istinggar* were made of brass. The stocks were like those of many European guns prior to 1600. They cannot be held to the shoulder properly. Old European illustrations show that these queerly shaped pieces were aimed and fired at arm's length in a forked rest, so probably the Malays did the same; or perhaps a shaped shoulder pad was worn to receive the kick.

Cartridges (*pĕtĕrum*) were made of sections of bamboo; powder flasks (*panggalah, kĕrpai*, or *kubit bĕdil*) were made of large seeds, or small gourds; they were also made of horn and gutta percha.[1]

---

[1] A genus of tropical tree (*Palaquium*), native to Southeast Asia, that provides high quality wood and also a valuable rubber latex sap. The name is derived from the Malay *getah perca*. (Ed.)

76. Detail of 75.

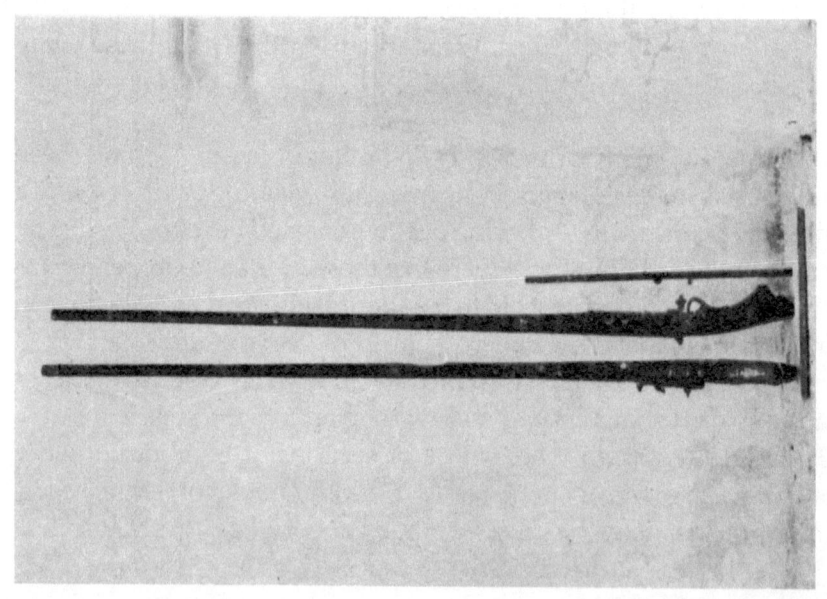

75. Matchlocks (Malay).

CHAPTER 6: SMALL ARMS

I have some flasks that are so small that they must have been used for priming powder. These made very ingenious bullet horns, so that one bullet at a time could be picked up quickly.

They also made bamboo covers bound with *rotan* to cover their guns in wet weather: (see Plate 74 No. 1a) and they made small mallets to drive the rifle balls down the barrel.[1]

Malays now use modern guns; but they are still very ingenious at making breechloading guns from old pipes with nails for striker, and rubber bands for springs, that will shoot 12-bore cartridges. They are also very ingenious in reloading cartridges: they hammer out the cap, line it with a bit of black striking-paper from a match box, fill it with crushed match heads, fill the cartridge case with powder from fireworks and use either slugs or chopped nails as shot. In Perak, some years ago, the Government made a boundary stone of cement with a lead disc on top, into which the number of land grant was stamped. The use of these had to be discontinued as the lead was all dug out for shot.

---

[1] See s. *pukol*.

CHAPTER 7

BOWS AND ARROWS

Many people say that Malays never used arrows, because they are not used to-day. I think they must have had them, though it is difficult to prove. The Javanese certainly used them and Malay literature contains many words used specifically in archery. For example:

panah: bow.
anak panah: arrow.
indong panah: quiver.
sayap: lit. wing: feathers of an arrow.
pikam: point of arrow.
bĕrgandi: to use the bow.
main gandi: archery.
anak panah kosong: headless arrow (for practice).

The blowpipe arrow is *anak sumpitan*. D'Albuquerque writing of the attack on Malacca says they were met with clouds of poisoned arrows. It is generally supposed that they were blowpipe arrows, because blowpipe arrows are always poisoned. I think, however, that had these been *anak sumpitan* d'Albuquerque would have said so, or at least referred to their smallness. An arrow was an everyday thing to him, and a blowpipe dart was not: moreover he was writing for people in Europe who did not know of blowpipes.

There is, however, one definite reference to the bow and arrow in Malay history. When the Portuguese were attacking Kota Kara in the time of Sultan Ala'udin Rayat Shah (1529-1564) there was a large tree that grew on the edge of the fort, and under a furious fire the Malays shot arrows with lines attached over the branches of this tree. They pulled up ropes with these and eventually pulled the whole tree over, effectually masking the Portuguese fire. These arrows

CHAPTER 7: BOWS AND ARROWS

must have been shot from a bow as it is impossible to shoot a line on a blowpipe arrow.

In the thick jungle a bow is rather unwieldy, while a blowpipe is not; and there is no wind in the jungle so the tiny darts fly true; but where there is wind an arrow shot from a bow being much heavier would go straight to the mark. The Malays being seafaring people would need a weapon that could be used in the wind.

The Malays met Chinese, Indians, Persians and other races who used bows, and I am sure, learned to use them also until guns were obtainable.

I have been asked why, if there were Malay bows, there are none to be seen now. I would point out that while the English bowman was famous throughout Europe, there are only four old English bows in existence, all the others having rotted away.

In the store room of Raffles Museum there is a fine specimen of a bamboo bow. This is either Malay or Javanese. From excavations in an old battlefield on the Johore River, I obtained two bronze articles which seem to be arrow heads; but though these may be Chinese, they are exactly like iron arrow heads in the Batavia Museum.

SUMPITAN (BLOWPIPE).

The *sumpitan* as used in Borneo has a wooden shaft from 6 to 8 feet long. It is usually made from a single tree trunk, which is bored out, then thinned down. The bore is polished by a rotan pull-through.

The making of a blowpipe is no easy task, and in spite of all the care taken, the finished tube is rarely quite straight. Advantage is taken of this, and a spear head of the exact weight to straighten the tube when the sight is uppermost, is fastened to the end.

The blowpipe with its spear is a very effectual weapon both as a missile weapon or as a spear (see Plate 78). The Sakai, Sĕmang, Jakun and other uncivilised tribes of the Malay Peninsula use a bamboo blowpipe.

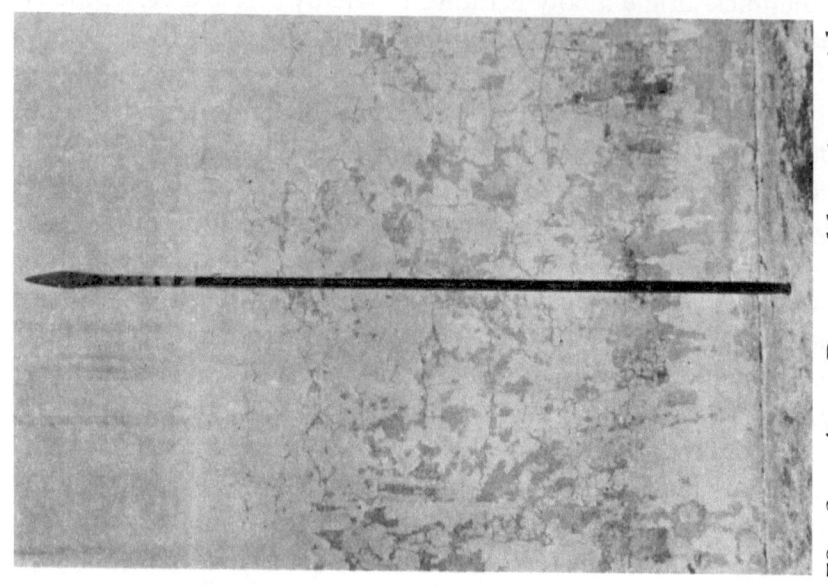

78. *Sumpitan*. Borneo blowpipe with spearhead attached to straighten tube. Mouthpiece rests on ground.

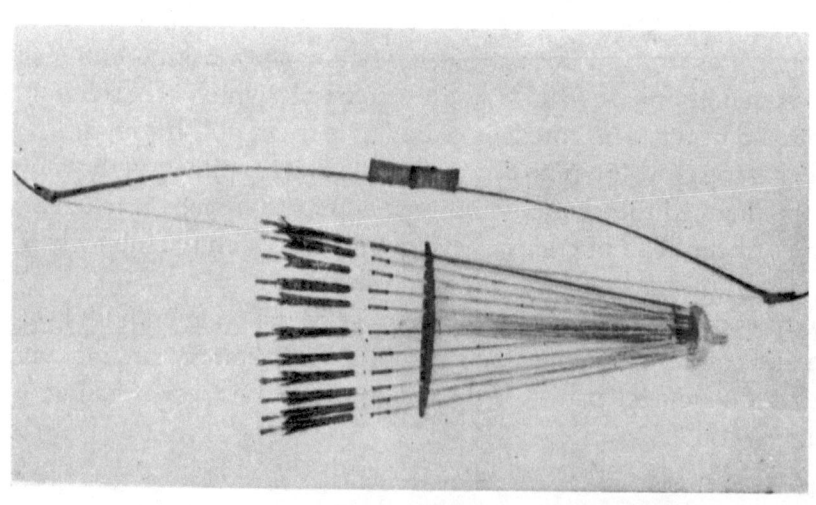

77. Javanese bow and arrows.

CHAPTER 8

MISCELLANEOUS WEAPONS

I MISCELLANEOUS OLD WEAPONS.

AXES.

In ancient times the inhabitants of the Malay Peninsula used various axes and adzes of stone, both rough and polished. These were certainly tools at first, though they may also have served as weapons. Some of the later polished stone axes were copies of bronze original and so cannot be very early. They are probably A.D. Possibly at that time these people possessed through trade, a few bronze axes, spears and knives and made copies of the axes and spears in stone. For the most part, however, they had to be content with wooden and bamboo spears, daggers of *ikan pari* and knives of split bamboo or stone. However until the country is properly excavated this must remain conjecture.

There are extant specimens of:

kapak: an iron axe or large sized hatchet.
kapak jĕpun: a pole axe (probably Japanese).
pĕpatil: a small adze.
rimbas: a small axe.

THROWING WEAPONS.

These are:
(1) A chain club.
(2) *batu rajut*.
(3) *chakira*.

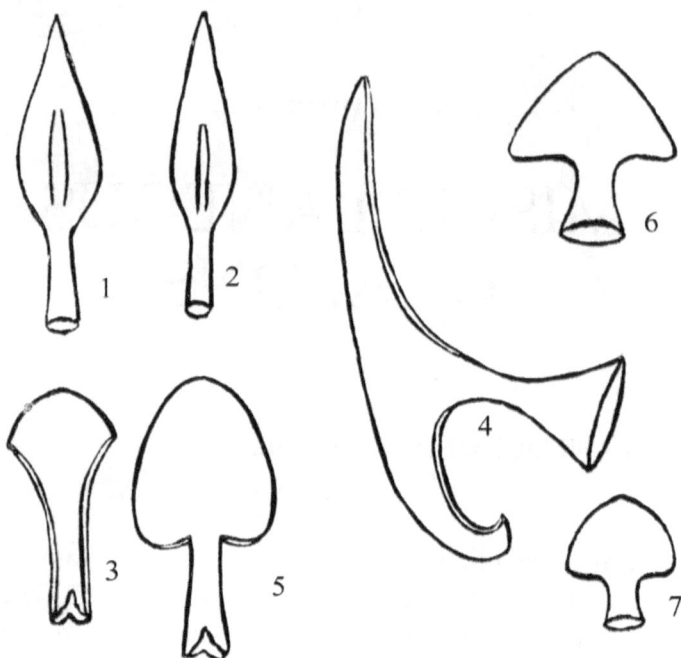

79. Ancient bronze weapons of Java. 1 & 2. Spears. 3 & 5. Axes. 4. Large axe. 6 & 7. May be halberds.

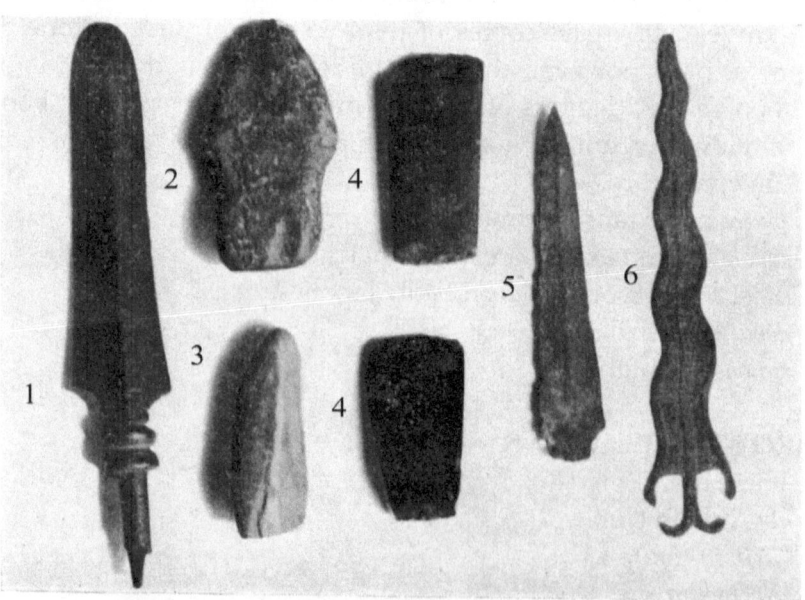

80. 1. Bronze spearhead with central ridge. 2. Stone age spearhead without ridge. 3. Stone spearhead; broken; Bronze or Iron Age copy of bronze or iron original with ridge. 4. Stone axeheads.

CHAPTER 8: MISCELLANEOUS WEAPONS

(1) The chain club is whirled (*baling baling*) to obtain momentum and then thrown. A light form is much used by Chinese jugglers and weapon players, but in ancient times it was a formidable weapon (see Plate 81 No. 1). This specimen is heavy and it takes a strong man to swing it for long. A similar weapon is the Indian chain sword.

(2) *batu rajut*: a metal ball bound in network and used as a missile. Wilkinson gives this as a Malay weapon but I have been unable to trace it. However, outside the fort, Kota Simpana, in Malacca, a brass ball was found. This was thought to be a cannon ball. Brass is a very expensive material of which to make cannon balls; and while it is possible that Malays finding that stone balls made no impression on stone walls, and being unable to make cast iron may have used brass for this purpose, I am inclined to think this may be one of the balls of which Wilkinson speaks. It might easily have been dropped during an attack (see Plate 81 No. 2).

I obtained a kind of *batu rajut* from a Chinese weapon player, which he called (in Chinese) *tim bing*. It is made of brass, having a peg with a hole to take a cord. This is about 16 feet long, with a loop on the end for the left wrist. In use the cord is looped loosely in the left hand: is grasped about 3 feet from the ball by the right hand, the ball is whirled round quickly to acquire momentum and released, the cord travelling through a loop formed by the right thumb and forefinger. As soon as the ball hits (or misses) its mark, is pulled back by the cord and whirled again for the next shot. To test this weapon I put up four bottles on a fence. The weapon player at a distance of fourteen feet broke each of them, then broke three planks in the fence, all with seven shots in sixteen seconds, He said it was a very old Chinese weapon, but it took a lot of practice before one could use it, and that if one were charged before one got up enough pace one used the ball as a club. I cannot be certain that the *batu rajut* was used in this way: but the Malays were fond of foreign weapons and copied them; so the *batu rajut* was probably copied from the *tim bing*. Why they did not make them with a hole to take the cord is a puzzle. I can only suggest that the origin of this weapon was a stone (*batu*: stone) and that when they used metal they made the weapon in the old form. In the British Museum are some British weapons: stones which have grooves worked round them to take a cord, and I believe they were used in much the same way.

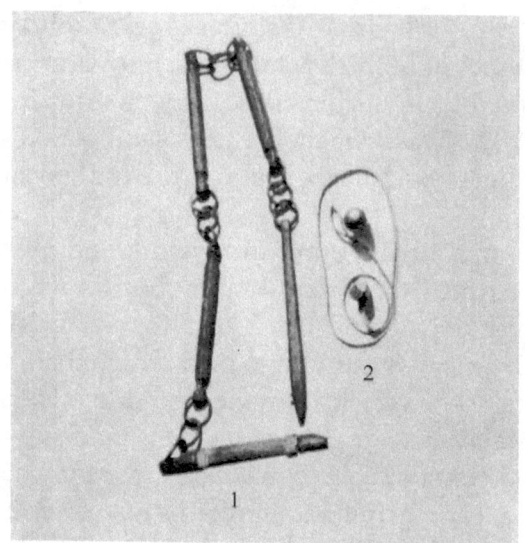

81. 1. *Baling-baling.*   2. *Batu rajut.*

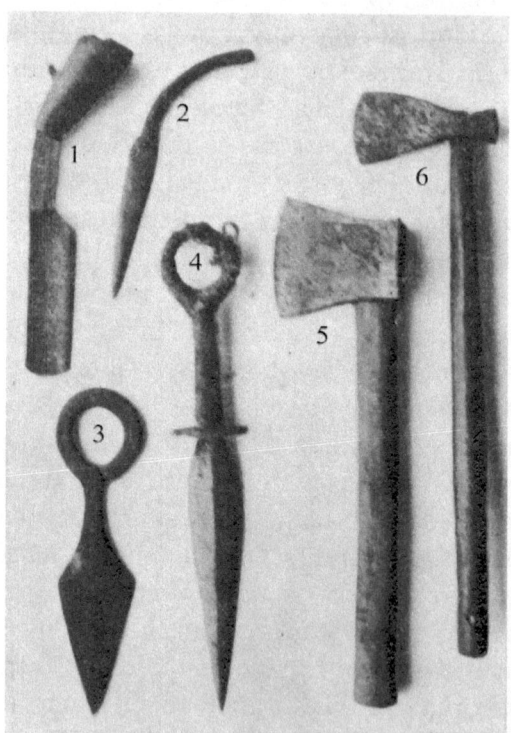

82. 1. Razor blade in *tumbok lada* hilt.   2. Brass stabbing knife.
3. A kind of knuckle duster.   4. Name uncertain, see text.   5 &
6. Stone axes.

(3) *chakira* is a war quoit with a serrated edge, mentioned in Malay writings and depicted on Javanese monuments. It is a well known Indian weapon, and I have no doubt the Malays used it, but so far I have been unable to find a specimen.

It is whirled round on the forefinger and thrown so as to skim through the air horizontally. It is said to be able to sever a man's neck, or the stem of a giant bamboo, at 50 yards. Wilkinson thinks the passage, *hujan panah dan chakĕra*, (a rain of arrows and war quoits) means a shower of arrows and discus-headed arrows, pointing out that Raffles illustrates a discus headed arrow. However, the weapon illustrated by Raffles would be useless in war, though it might probably kill birds.

The following slings and catapults are known to have been used:
ati-ali a catapult, usually made of leather or plaited *rotan*, on which the missile is placed. Also a sling.
umban tali a sling made from fibrous bark, sometimes of human hair.

CLUBS.
tĕmbong: a quarter staff or long cudgel.
tĕmbong kimboja: a short cudgel.
toyah: a thrusting pole for use in a scrimmage.
gayong: a kind of quarter staff. In romances it has magic powers and multiplies blows: if it hits, one is hurt in two places, if it misses, one is hurt in one.
pinang layar: (" Penang lawyer ") cudgel made from the wood of the *Pinang liar*.
chokmar: a mace, or spiked club, known only in romances.
gada: a warclub, but not a mace.
gada limbang: knuckle duster (from W. Sumatra).
pĕnumbak tĕmbaga: *brass* knuckle duster.

OTHER WEAPONS.
panah ayer: a squirt or syringe. This was used with the poisonous sap of the *buta buta* tree (*buta*: blind) in order to blind the enemy.
sĕreng: a fire raising arrow or rocket.

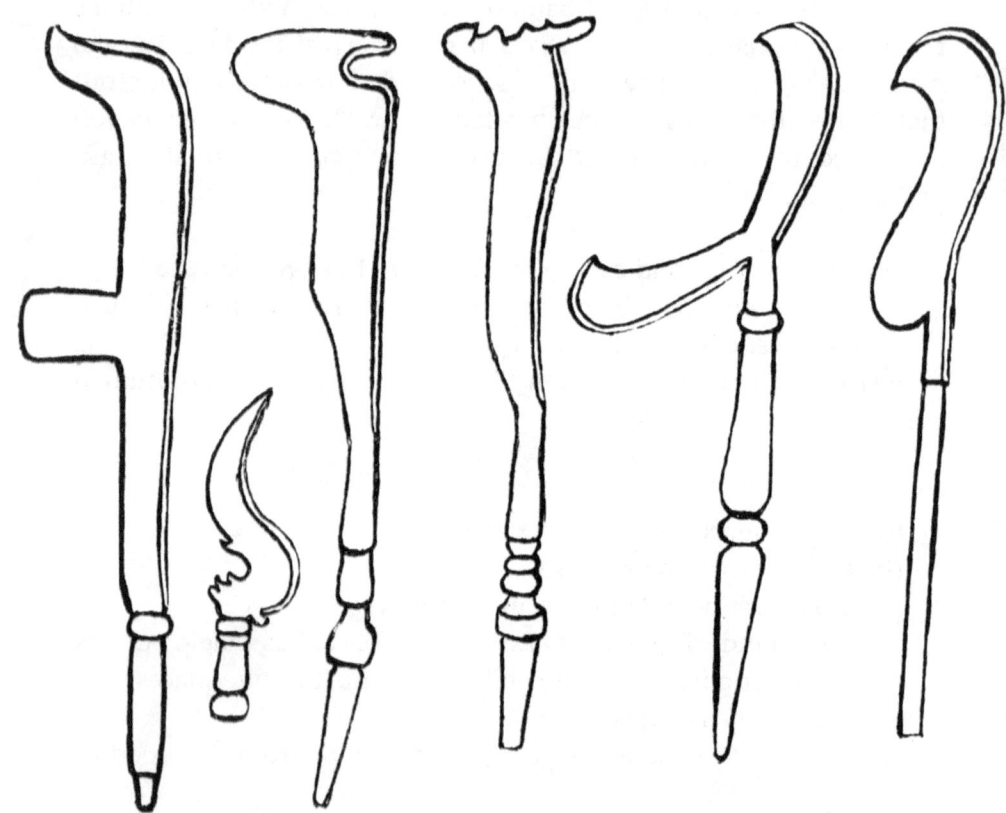

83. *Kudi* (various). These ancient weapons were used both as weapons and as agricultural implements until quite recently in Java.

CHAPTER 8: MISCELLANEOUS WEAPONS

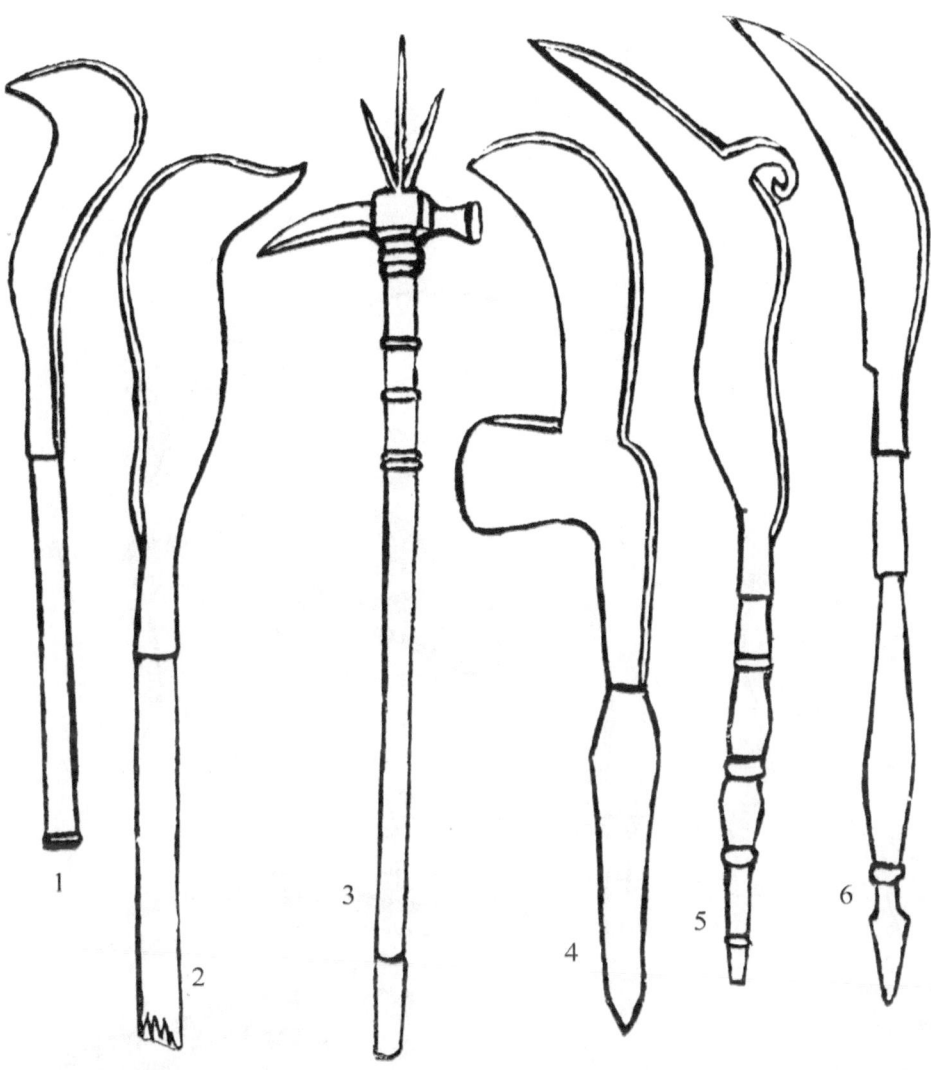

84. Old weapons from E. Java. 1 & 2. *Ruding lengong*. 3. *Kapak jĕpun*. 4, 5 & 6. *Kudi*. (Note: weapons not all in same scale).

tekpi: an iron weapon with a large guard, and a blunt point. It was used for parrying and also was a weapon, either for thrusting at the stomach, spleen or face, or as a club. It could be used to evade a law against carrying sharp weapons. Chinese, but used by Malays.

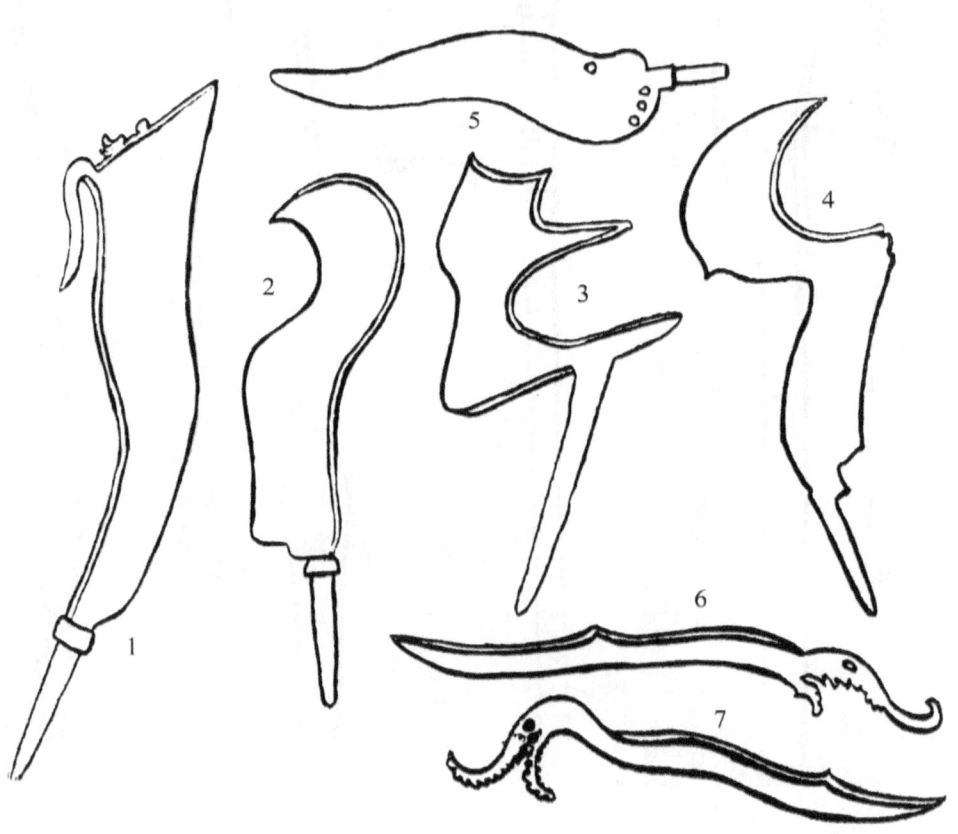

85. Ancient weapons. 1-4. *Kudi*.   5. Spearhead.   6 & 7. Knives.

II MISCELLANEOUS MODERN WEAPONS

When the Malays were disarmed they were permitted to carry *parang*, which are agricultural implements. Some ingenious people made heavy *kĕris* blades, and fitted them into *parang* hilts and sheaths. They could be used for chopping, but were really *kĕris*. I have been given a name *rebong* (shoot of bamboo) for these but am not certain if this is a general or only a local name. Other evaders of the law had small axe heads fitted with short handles, that could be carried in a side pocket. The hammers used for breaking road metal were often stolen and one end forged into an axe edge to make such weapons. Thirty years ago these were frequently carried in Perak, and I have known them used with drastic results (see Plate 82 Nos. 5 & 6).

A nasty ripping knife is sometimes made by fixing an old razor blade into a *tumbok lada* hilt. The shape of this hilt makes the blade project when held as a *lawi ayam* and an upward slash at the stomach or a cut at the neck is deadly (see Plate 82 No. 1).

Small knife blades four to five inches long, often of European manufacture are fitted with hilts and loose wooden scabbards. These are carried in side pockets. The sheath is intentionally loose so that it would drop off if the knife were hurriedly drawn.

Another knife has a loop at the top for the forefinger like a *lawi ayam*. It is poniard shaped, with a small guard, all forged out of a single piece of iron. The hilt and ring are wrapped round with string to give a better grip. The ring prevents the knife being wrested from the band. It is probably made by a Chinese blacksmith, for Malays, and looks home made (see Plate 82 No. 4).

I cannot discover any name except *pisau* (knife) for the last three types.

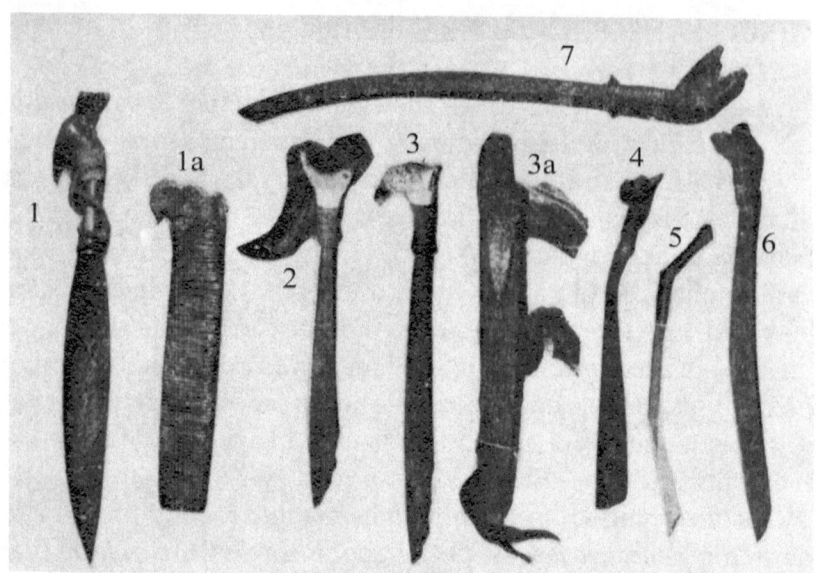

86. 1 & 1a. *Bajau běladau* and sheath. 2. *P. ilang*. 3 & 3a. *P. ilang* and sheath. 4. *Latok buku*. 5. Small *latok buku* (tool). 6. *Parang pědang*. 7. *Pakayun* (Murut).

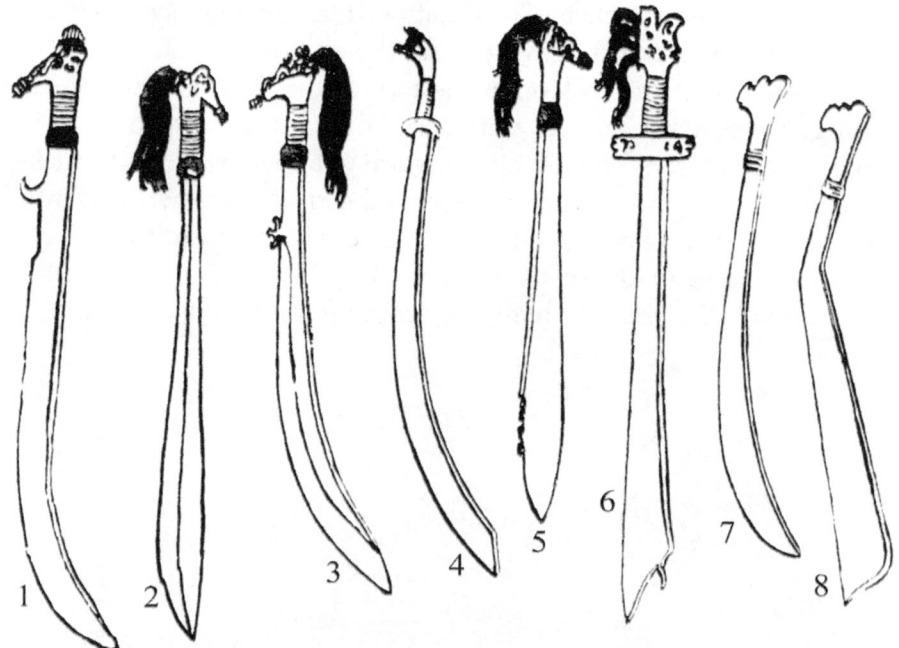

87. 1. *Naibor*. 2. *Bayu*. 3. *Langgi tinggang*. 4. *Pakayun*. 5. *Parang ilang*. 6. *Kělewang*. 7. *Parang pědang*. 8. *Latok buku*.

CHAPTER 9

DAYAK WEAPONS

The *parang* of the Dayak and other tribes of Borneo seem to be adapted from the Malay swords. I therefore include them.

The Sea Dayak use the following varieties:
- (1) *naibor*.
- (2) *langgai tinggang*.
- (3) *jumbul*.
- (4) *baju*.

(1) The *naibor* is a curved scimitar. The back and edge curve to a point without any slope. There is a large finger guard. The hilt is often made of stag's horn. This is cut to form a good sized hilt: the brow tine is cut to form a sort of hook and usually carved. The *naibor* is not decorated with tufts of hair as the *parang ilang* is (q.v.).

(2) The *langgai tinggang* is a *naibor* with a broad groove cut out on each side of the blade from the finger guard to point. The name means the tail of a hornbill, which this groove is supposed to resemble.
The finger guard is much smaller than that of the *naibor* and set further down the blade, and it has a *parang* hilt like a *parang ilang*.

(3) The *jumbul* looks like a *parang ilang* but is not concave or convex and is slightly curved.

(4) The *baju* is a double edged weapon, looks like a *parang ilang* but is neither concave nor convex.
   These blades are often incised with very beautiful patterns and are of very good steel. They are sometimes decorated by boring holes in the blade and inserting brass pegs (*lantak paku*).

The sheaths of all these Borneo swords are made of two pieces of wood hollowed out and fastened together with *rotan*, brass or silver wire lashings. An exception is the Murut sword which is fastened with strips of tin. The Muruts are said not to be able to make *sampir*. Their sheaths are often beautifully carved and decorated with bone, shell and hair.

The Land Dayak use:
(1) *buku*: A small weapon., usually made by bending a square bar of iron at a slight angle, and, forging the longer end into a broad ended blade. It has a hilt like the *parang pědang*.
(2) *pandat*: the fighting *parang*, it is like the *buku* but has no wooden hilt; instead, the iron shoulder is made longer and a hole bored through to take an iron bar which forms a cross guard.

The Borneo Malays use:
(1) *parang pědang*: the blade is long, curved and broad at the end tapering nearly to a point at the hilt. The blade is not ornamented and the hilt is of wood; it is used mostly for agriculture, but can be an effective weapon.
(2) *latok*: a large form of the *buku*. It is heavy and used with both hands.

The Kayan, Kenya, Kelabit, Punan and Pulong. These tribes use:
(1) *parang ilang*: has a blade that is concave on the inner, side, the side towards the user, convex on the outer. This is to make it cut inward, cutting downward at an angle of forty-five degrees. Used on a small tree the *parang ilang* will turn slightly and cut through, while an ordinary shaped blade would, through the splitting of the wood, tend to cut downward and not through; and thus would take two or three cuts to do what the *parang* will do in one. It is said that with downward cut at an angle of forty-five degrees the weapon will turn enough to cut a man's head clean off.

This peculiarity of the blade makes it dangerous for a novice to use; as if the stroke is not made at the exact angle it tends to turn in the hand, or fly back, striking the user with the edge. As the concavity is not always the same even an adept has to learn to use a new *parang ilang*.

A left handed man has the concave and convex edges reversed, so that the weapon will always cut in towards the bearer.

In the Philippines *parang* are used that are sharpened only on the outer edge and which thus have something of the same cutting effect

Murut.

The only weapon which is peculiar to the Murut is the *pakayun*. This has a long narrow, curved blade, without ornamentation. The hilt is of wood, carved with a design of two pigs. The grip is usually a brass tube expanding into a lip, which forms a finger guard.

APPENDIX A

MALAY WARFARE

From Marsden's *History of Sumatra* (1811) we learn that the spirit of war was excited among the Malays on the smallest provocation. They appeared in fact to be in a state of perpetual hostility and they were always prepared for attack or defence. Between the Měnangkabau people and those of Riau and Acheh, warfare was incessant until it was checked by the British.

Although much parade attended their preparations of war, yet their operations were carried on rather in the way of ambuscade and surprise of straggling parties, than open combat: firing irregularly from behind entrenchments, which the enemy took care not to approach.

The first act of defiance was firing, without ball, into the *kampong* of the enemy. Three days were allowed for the party fired upon to propose terms of accommodation. If this were not done or the terms could not be agreed upon, war was fully declared. During the course of the war which sometimes lasted for two or three years they seldom met openly in the field or attempted to decide the contest by a general engagement as the mutual loss of a dozen might go near to ruin both parties, nor did they ever engage hand to hand, but fired at extreme range.

Nevertheless they were not fond of remaining on the defensive in fortified places, but preferred to advance into the plain and throw up temporary breast-works and embankments.

The soldiers served without pay. The plunder was thrown into the common stock and divided among them. They marched in single file and usually fired kneeling.

They were said to go to war on horseback; but, while the chiefs might have used horses for purposes of display, on account of the *ranjau* or pointed stakes planted in the passes they could not have been employed effectively.

Their campaigns were carried out with great deliberation. They made a regular practice of a truce at sunset, when they remained for the night in mutual security; and they sometimes agreed that hostilities should take place between certain hours of the day only. The English Resident, Mr. Carter, was frequently chosen as their umpire and used to fix a spot where the deputies should meet and discuss terms.

Marsden did not approve of the Malay way of making warfare, and did not understand it. To the Malay, war was a game, something to break the monotony. Nowadays the idea of war is something horrible and as such, to be finished as soon as possible. Malay war was different; it was waged in a spirit of sport and emulation so why should it not be made reasonably comfortable? Hence the very sensible agreements to cease fighting at sunset so that both sides could eat and sleep in peace.

War was an exciting pastime for a man. If he were unlucky he withdrew to fight again; if he were lucky there were both loot and women for the taking. It should be mentioned here that *gundek jarahan* (a mistress taken in war) was a position which entailed no disgrace.

The Hikayat Bugis tells a delightful incident of an army taunted in a very gross way (*luchun*) to provoke it to attack a very strong position: *'běrpěrang sěpěrti di-luchun orang sahaja, di-běri orang burit dan pantat-lah.'* (The army in question did not enjoy this, and being too prudent to attack at disadvantage, returned home).

The Malays have a curious description of what a soldier should be: *lari ta'-malu, běrhambat ta'lugu* (not ashamed to run away, not too self-satisfied to pursue). This sounds strange to us; but, in a country of dense jungle, a man can do much more for his side by guerrilla tactics than by getting killed defending a forlorn hope.

Marsden gives an account of an expedition in 1804. Lieut. Hastings Dare was sent to chase Malays who had raided Ipu, one of the East India Company's districts and burnt several villages and carried off many of the inhabitants. He had 83 sepoys, officers and men, 5 lascars, 22 Bengal convicts and 18 of the Bugis guard. He marched through the hills for many days and had many men wounded in the feet by *ranjau*. These are slips of bamboo, sharpened at each end. The part that is stuck in the ground is thicker; the opposite end decreases to a thin point, which is hardened by dipping in oil and applying to the smoke of a lamp near the flame. They are planted in the foot paths, sometimes erect sometimes sloping in small holes or in muddy and miry places and when trodden upon, for they are well concealed and not to be seen, they pierce the foot and make a most disagreeable wound. The bamboo, leaving in the wound the rough hairs from its bark, irritates, inflames and prevents it healing. Here is Lieut. Dare's rather laconic account:

> "Reached a spot very difficult to pass being knee deep in mud for a considerable way and spring spears set in many places, bombarded the fort with a mortar... and commenced attack, but were unable for a number of *ranjau* in only accessible part, to make a push at the enemy. However, at one o'clock, we outflanked them and got complete possession of the embankment which, had it been properly defended must have cost us more than half our detachment. We had four sepoys wounded and almost the whole of our feet badly cut. Numbers of the enemy were killed and wounded. They defended each of their batteries with some obstinacy against our fire but when we came near they could not stand our arms and ran in every direction... Attacking another fort, they found a number of trees felled to obstruct the road, attacked scrambling over the trees and with great difficulty got the mortar over, our men were dropping fast, not being able to advance on account of the *ranjau* which almost pinned their feet to the ground, tried a flank attack and when this developed a general attack they were soon put to rout, and lost great numbers, among them their leader. We lost two sepoys, killed, seven wounded and several more hurt by *ranjau*."

APPENDIX B

MALAY WAR DRESS

The articles of war dress are:
(1) *Chĕlana*: These are pantaloons buttoned from hip to ankle.
(2) *Katok*: A short kilt or petticoat of coloured silk or fine cotton, ending just below the knee.
(3) *Sabok*: A length of silk or fine cotton rolled tightly round the body like a military sash seven or eight times, and extending from the armpits to the hips.
(4) *Sangsang*: A tight vest with the buttons worn over the *sabok*.
(5) *Kotau*: Another vest buttoning round the body to the neck, worn over the sangsang.
(6) *Sikapan*: A jacket worn over the whole.
(7) *Tali-pĕdang*: This is a sword belt worn round the waist and supporting the sword on the left.
(8) *Tudong*: A shade for the face.
(9) Shoes or sandals are generally worn.

Three *kĕris* are usually worn, one on each side and one at the back. These consists of the wearer's own *kĕris*, the *kĕris* that has descended to him from his ancestors, and the *kĕris* which he may have received in marriage from his wife's father, which is on the left side for immediate use. This dress is for battle, and it is the custom to wear the richest attire that means permit, and to wear rings and other valuables.

ARMOUR.
Malays have never used much armour, as it is known in Europe.

The following specimens, however, are extant:
(1) *Baju rantai* or *baju bĕsi*: Iron coat of chain mail probably obtained

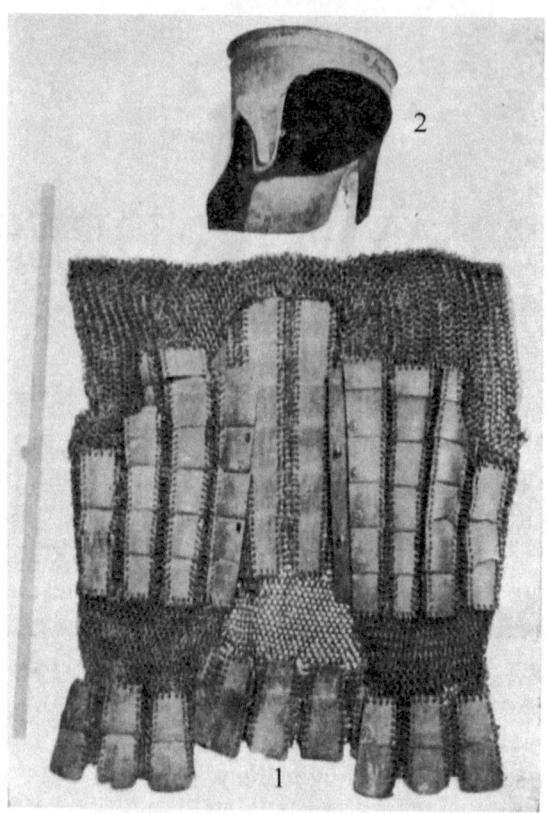

88. 1. *Baju lamina.*   2. *Kěchubong,* helmet.

89. *Baju rantai* or *běsi.*

from the Portuguese, as these are too large for most Malays (see Plate 89).
(2) *Baju lamina*: A native made coat of mail of brass rings. These also have oblong scales of brass or horn in front and behind (see Plate 88).
(3) *Kĕchubong*: Brass helmets made in imitation of those used in Europe and India. These are rare.
(4) *Utah*: Round wooden shields sometimes having ornamental metal plates.
(5) *Tameng*: round shields of basket work covered with leather or cloth, often having small metal stars or spikes. This type of shield was occasionally made of brass.
(6) *Rangin*: long shields of Indonesian type, covered with a thin gold plate (*sarong pĕrisai mas*) as a mark of rank.
(7) *Utah-utah*: Small shields hung with bells and streamers were used in war dances.
(8) Broad wadded belts were also used as a protection (see Plate 90).

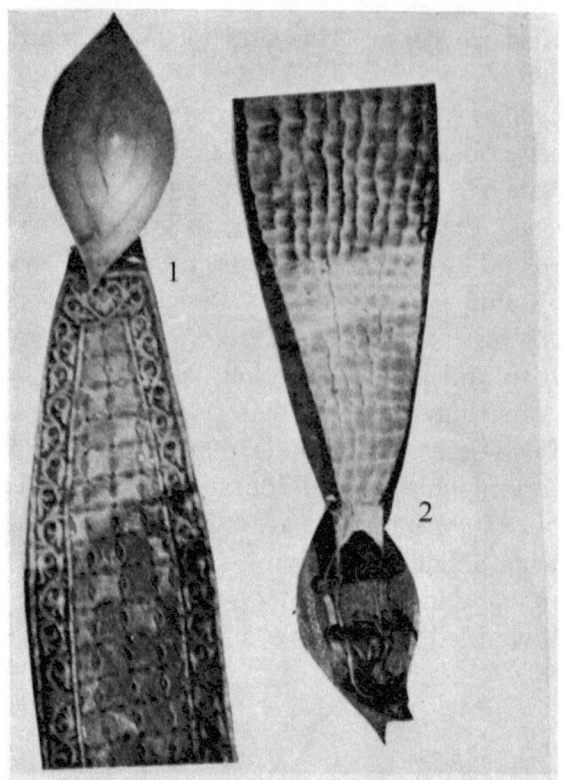

90. 1. Protective wadded belt (½ length). 2. Same reversed

91. *Tameng,* shield.

APPENDIX C

MALAY FORTIFICATIONS

Malay war seems to have been mostly an affair of outposts. The fact was that against primitive weapons, the forts on either hills or in the midst of swamps defended by *ranjau* were almost impregnable. Though Malays had heavy artillery and some of the stone balls found embedded in the walls of the old forts are 8½ inches in diameter, still a stone ball of this size has not the weight of an iron ball and would not make the slightest impression on an earth rampart, and very little on one of heavy logs.

They were, therefore, obliged to make war by quick raids and by cutting off small parties of the enemy. When Europeans came with mortars and shells it was different. An earth wall that would keep out forty cannon balls was no protection against one mortar that would lob shells over it.

Malay forts in the Peninsula, being constructed mostly of earth and timber have practically disappeared in the course of time; while where stone was used, it has been taken away and used for building.

Marsden in his *History of Sumatra* says:

"They fortify their *kampongs* with large ramparts of earth, half way up which they plant brushwood; there is a ditch without a rampart and on each side of that a tall palisade of camphor timber; beyond this is an impenetrable hedge of prickly bamboo which when of sufficient growth acquires an exceeding density, and perfectly conceals the town. *Ranjau* of a length both for the body and the feet are disposed without all these and render the approaches hazardous to the assailants who are almost naked. At each corner of the fortress instead of a tower, they contrive to have a tall tree which they ascend to reconnoitre or fire from."

The entrenchments were constructed of large trees laid horizontally between sticks about 7 feet high driven into the ground with loopholes for firing; and being laid about 6 feet thick, were impenetrable to cannon.

Marsden goes on to say:

"(we)... attacked Kota Tunggoh; the inhabitants fled on our throwing in one shell and firing a few muskets. It is situated on a high hill nearly perpendicular on three sides. The easiest entrance was defended by a ditch, seven fathoms deep and five fathoms wide."

A curious feature of nearly every old Malay fort is that while it had strong defences of ditches and ramparts in front and minor defences at the sides, the rear was left apparently undefended. The explanation is that these forts faced the river and were surrounded by jungle. The defenders had to have a place for their own boats to land and built a fort to defend it; the river was the only highway and the enemy must, therefore, approach from that quarter. Before the general use of small arms it was impossible to make a flank attack through defended jungle without terrible loss of life: since no cannon could be brought through jungle and the ground would be planted with *ranjau*. The trees would be full of armed men and the attackers would be subjected to a continuous rain of spears and stones from the tree tops. These, projected from a height of 40-50 feet, would fall with terrific force, while the defenders would be well hidden.

The following are terms generally used in connection with fortifications and defence:

Kota: a permanent fort: strictly speaking should have stone work.

susur kota: the outer walls of the fort.

kubu: a stockade: semi-permanent, strengthened with earth and ditches. The only *kubu* I have seen had a wall of squared tree trunks, about 14 feet high; it was in a state of decay, but when in its prime would probably have been proof against all but the heaviest native artillery.

chělěngkoh: a bastion or turret at the corner of a fort.

pěnampang: level top of parapet used as a gun platform.

bentong: breastworks or field fortifications, thrown up as needed.

ranggas: spiky mass of fallen timber used in front of *bentong*.

baluarti: a bulwark, rampart or fortified wall.

pagar: a palisade. Dutch accounts of about 1600 say the fort at Makam Tongkah a palisade of tree trunks 40 feet high. This was later taken by the Achehnese (1620).

ranjau: caltrop. Varieties are as follows:

(1) *ranjau běsi*: *chevaux-de-frise* of iron.

borong (Javanese) *chevaux-de-frise* made of three bamboo spears in the form of a tripod.

(2) *ranjau mata tiga*: a three pointed caltrop one point always uppermost.

ranjau mata satu: one pointed caltrop on a flat base.

(3) *ranjau ranchang*: any spiky obstruction fixed in the ground to prevent a rush.

(4) *ranjau pěnunggul*: Caltrop long enough to wound in the body instead of in the feet.

pělantek: a spring spear trap, set in the approach to a fort.

těrkepong: to lay siege to a fort.

APPENDIX D

INVULNERABILITY

Malays have always had great faith in charms against wounds and the use of magic weapons or talismanic metal. That the older Malays implicitly believe in these charmings there is ample proof.

About six years ago in Batu Pahat, Johore, there was an inquiry into the death of a man who stabbed himself in the breast in the presence of many witnesses. It transpired that he had been paying attentions to his neighbour's wife and that the husband had threatened him. He therefore went to the local *pawang*, who for a fair sum proceeded to make him invulnerable, a process that took several days. At the end of this time the *pawang* gave him a *kĕris* and said; "Stab yourself, the blade will not pierce." He did so and the *kĕris* did not harm him, but when he tried to repeat the performance to show off to his friends, it killed him. The *pawang* gave evidence in court that he had made many men, invulnerable, and it had always worked before, and he could not account for its failing this time, unless an evil spirit had been present.

About two years later I read in the paper of an almost identical case in Malacca, only in this case, the charmed man boasted to his friends and challenged them, and one of them hit him with a big felling axe, and split his skull.

I met two 'invulnerable' men both in Borneo, more than 25 years ago. The first a Dayak, had 17 scars of bullet and spears that had just grazed him he said and that his immunity was natural and that he had not practised any charms. Bullets would clip his skin but could not penetrate. I think he firmly believed it, and he certainly bad been lucky.

The second was a Bundu Dusun, who was in a small way a *pawang*. He practiced magic and said he had made himself invulnerable. He had a extraordinary scar encircling his upper right arm. He said a man had cut at him with a heavy *parang* which had passed right through his arm without severing it. The scar looked exactly as if this had happened, but I fancy he had made it himself to enhance his reputation. His neighbours believed him to be invulnerable but they said he was not much use as a *pawang*.

Years ago in Muar I was told a story of an 'invulnerable' man who was retained by the Sultan of Malacca as a sort of show. Anyone could shoot at him who liked, and one could see the bullets popping off him; but when the Sultan of Johore sent a man, with a golden bullet[1], the golden bullet killed him.

Invulnerability was sometimes claimed by people not, shall we say, 'entitled' to it. The late Mr. Cyril Blair Cooper told me of an amusing case that he witnessed 20 years ago in Batu Pahat. A man who had a grievance attempted to murder a high Malay official in the public street; the official parried the first thrust with his umbrella and said sternly: "Don't do, that you fool, you'll only spoil your *kĕris*. Don't you know I'm invulnerable?" and the assailant slunk off without calling his bluff.

Invulnerability is conferred:
(1) By the use of certain objects, which are in themselves talismanic (*azimat*).
  (a) *kĕlambu rasul Allah* (the Prophet's bed curtain) a sleeveless fighting jacket embroidered with pious texts.
  (b) *kĕris bĕrtuwah*: these, especially *k. majapahit* and *k. pichit* conferred on their owners *pĕrambut sĕnjata* or invulnerability to weapons.
  (c) *baju leher* (neck coat) a fighting jacket made of the 44 remnants left in cutting out the necks of 44 ordinary jackets. This jacket must be sewn together by seven maidens on seven consecutive Fridays; if the wearer has the misfortune to be killed, it is evidence of the frailty of one of the seven.
  (d) *sampul*: a caul. A child born with a complete caul is invulnerable.

---

[1] Grahame of Claverhouse, Viscount Dundee ('Bonnie' Dundee of the song) is said to have been killed with a silver bullet, though supposed to have been otherwise invulnerable.

(e) *běsi kuning* (lit. yellow iron): a legendary metal, probably bronze. It is always said to be harder than iron and a good bronze weapon would probably be harder than a primitive iron one. I possess an ancient bronze blade that is said to be *běsi kuning* but this claim is not admitted by most Malays who have seen it as they very sensibly say; "We have never seen *běsi kuning* only heard of it, and don't know what it looks like. The only way to test it, is to wear it and get someone to shoot at you, at close range, and if it prevents your being hurt it is *běsi kuning*." I have not made this test yet. (See Pl. 80 No. 5).

A weapon of *běsi kuning* is talismanic not only in defence but in attack also. *Běsi kuning* is by some said to be a single metal, but the most common theory is that it is an alloy of seven metals; of gold, silver, copper, tin, lead, iron and one other unknown metal.[1] The reason for this is that while a man may be charmed against some of the metals, one of the other, e.g. gold or silver, will kill him.

A weapon made *of běsi kuning* is not to be confused with the bronze and brass *kěris* and spear heads that are sometimes made nowadays. These may be partly for show, but I think there is not much doubt they are chiefly made to kill people who are supposed to be charmed against iron, steel or lead; i.e. cutting and thrusting weapons and bullets. I have a *kěris* from Kělantan the blade of which is covered with copper in small lumps, welded on, this entirely spoils the look of the *kěris*. I was told it was specially prepared to kill a certain man who was charmed in the usual way, and that it had done so.

(2) By the use of incantations (*jampi*) and drugs (*ubat*). This is of two kinds:
  (a) *pakan*, which renders hostile weapons impotent.
  (b) *kěbal*, which confers impenetrability.

(a) *pakan*. The art of securing this is called *ilmu pěrapoh* or *ilmu pěnyala*; *pakan* will paralyse an enemy's arm, or cause his weapons to become brittle and break. *Pakan* also makes

---

[1] See also the theory that the more kinds of iron the better the *kěris*.

weapons miss altogether. The method is referred to in Hikayat Anggun: '*di-běri makan ubat pakan sakalian-nya*' (he fed them on drugs that made them invulnerable).

Each metal has to be charmed against separately, by a *pawang* who knows its secret name and nature. This process takes time and money; therefore, only common metals are usually charmed against, e.g. iron and lead. Such a charm would be of no use against, say, a k. *majapahit,* because it is made of *majapahit* iron, of which no one now knows the nature. Moreover, such a *kĕris* would have its own *sĕmangat* or indwelling spirit, which is stronger than any magic. A charm against iron or lead would be useless against a bronze weapon: for another fee a man could be made proof against bronze; but gold and silver are especially potent; and it is very difficult if not impossible to charm against them.

These are the impressions I have gathered from questioning old people. They know endless tales and legends but are unable to be definite on any point.

(b) *kĕbal.* The art of conferring *kĕbal* is called *ilmu kibal*: a study of *ilmu kĕbal* was part of the education of every hero of romance or history. The impenetrability is of several kinds:
(1) *kĕbal kulit*: hardening the skin, making it like that of a toad (*kĕbal katak puru*).
(2) *kĕbal minyak*: making the skin slippery, as if with oil (*minyak*), so that weapons glance off.
(3) *kĕbal pĕnimbul*: protecting the flesh by rubbing quicksilver into the body so as to get a subcutaneous metallic armour; the idea is that the quicksilver rushes at once to the wound and so prevents further penetration.

The word *kĕbal* is sometimes used incorrectly for *pakan*.

sangga bunoh is a charm against death in battle.

PĔLURU TUNANG.

In addition to personal invulnerability prowess in warfare is sought by the use of charmed bullets (*pĕluru*). A bullet is charmed by incantations (*bĕrjampi*) until it becomes *tunang* (guaranteed to reach its mark). My informants were uncertain whether it would penetrate any of the above mentioned defences of invulnerability: so the problem of what would happen if it were used against *pakan* or *kĕbal* remains unsolved. It would seem to be the old case of the irresistible force meeting the immovable object. Some say that the outcome would depend on the relative powers of the *pawang* who had charmed the bullet, and of the one who had conferred the invulnerability.

It is generally supposed that against *ilmu pĕnyala*, *pĕluru tunang* will shatter, and while not lethal, will do considerable damage. All agree that a gold bullet, and to a less degree a silver one, will penetrate any invulnerability.

NOTE: The gold bullet superstition is unknown in Europe but the silver bullet recurs frequently in history and romance. It was commonly supposed that certain highwaymen were charmed against steel, lead and hemp. In the middle of the eighteenth century an Irish highwayman, who was supposed to have such a charm, was hanged eight times, and broke the rope each time. The ninth time he was successfully hanged with a chain. Why the charm did not work against iron is not related.

GLOSSARY

NOTE: Nearly all these words have been verified in Wilkinson's Malay-English Dictionary; 2nd. edition, 1932; there are, however, some Javanese and Dayak words which Mr. Gardner uses, of which it has been impossible to verify either the spelling or the meaning. This is so noted in the glossary; but an explanation or illustration will usually be found in the text. (BLM)

A.

Acheh, Achin	a state in Sumatra.
ada	the verb to be in all forms: there are no inflections.
agong	1. great or important 2. bump against head.
alang	medium.
ali-ali	sling; catapult.
anak	child; offspring; young.
api	fire; flame; light.
aring	fretted work under pointed end of *ganja*.
atas	above; over.
ayam	fowl.
ayer	water.
azimat	talismanic.

B.

badan	body.
badek	a kind of *kĕris*.
bahari	*kĕris* with long narrow blade.
baluarti	rampart.
bangkong	heavy (of weapons).
bantal	cushion.
bajau	sea-gipsy; Dyak tribe.
baju	1. coat 2. Dyak weapon.
bari	see note on p. 9.

barong	Filipino word for *parang*.
batir-batir	gold loop ornament thro' which passes the *tuli-tuli* of a *kěris*.
batu	stone.
baur	Perak sword of office.
bawang	bulb shaped hilt of *kěris*.
bědil	firearms (generic).
beka	broad and rounded; *buah b.* a fruit so shaped.
běkang	open; wide-ended.
běladau	curved, single-edged dagger
Bělalai	elephant's trunk.
bělerang	sulphur.
bělukar	secondary jungle; undergrowth.
běnděrang	*tombak b.* tufted spear.
bengkok	crooked; bent.
benteng	breastwork.
běntok	curved.
běrandal	heavy Borneo sword.
běrhambat	to pursue; to harry.
běri	bestowal; to give.
běrlok	sinuous (of *kěris*).
běrjol	Javanese weapon.
běrkait	hooked.
běrpamor	damascened.
běrperarg	to make war.
běrtimbal	double ended.
běrtupai	sword with guard to hilt.
běrtuwah	luck-bringing.
běsi	iron.
buah	fruit.
buang	discard.
Bugis	coast communities of Celebes.
buloh	bamboo.
bunga	flower, flower pattern.
bunoh	kill.
buntu	closed to ingress.
buntut	tail-end; stern.
burit	stern; posterior.
buta	blind.

CH.
chakak	grip; struggle.
chakĕra	quoit.
chakok	billhook.
champak	discard.
chandak	short stabbing spear.
chandong	hilt and blade in one piece; unbarbed.
changkok	pointed.
chĕlaka	unlucky; accursed.
chĕlana	fighting trousers.
chĕlengkoh	bastion.
chĕnangkas	straight edged sword.
chĕriga	short broad sword; cf. *tjoeriga*.
chĕrita	*kĕris* with 9 or more bends.
chinchin	finger ring.
choban	needle.
chokmar	mace.
chundĕrik	chopper.
chura si manjakini	name of dynastic sword.

D.
daga	small *kĕris* (from Eng: 'dagger')
daripada	from; arising out of.
dayak	upcountry; the Dayak are people of the interior.
dĕmam	fever.
dĕmang	title of Javanese chief.
di	in; at; as result of.
dua	two.

E.
ĕmas	gold.
ĕmbalau	shellac.
ĕmpunya	possession; to own.
ekur	tail.

G.
gabus	highly tempered; *k. tĕrapang g.* gold sheathed *kĕris*.
gada	war club.

gading	ivory.
gajah	elephant.
galaganjar	state halberd.
gandi	a bow.
bĕrgandi	archery.
ganja	guard on *kĕris* blade.
gayong	singlestick; supposed to have magic powers.
gĕdubang	heavy short sword.
gĕganit	bayonet.
golok	machete; sword.
gondok	squat; short.
gundek	mistress.

H.

harubi	*k. harubi;* gold hilted *kĕris.*
hujong	point; tip.
hulu	bead; hilt; hinterland.

I.

ikan	fish; *i. pari* sting ray.
ilang	(Dayak).
Ilanun	Moro, Sulu & all N. Borneo pirates.
ilmu	any branch of knowledge or magic.
indong	mother.
iras	original material.
istinggar	flintlock or matchlock gun.

J.

jabong	glue.
jahat	evil.
jalar	to crawl sinuously.
jambiah	curved dagger.
jambu-jambu	crest, tuft or ball on helmet or standard.
jampi	magic by incantations.
janggut	beard.
jantan	male.
jarahan	prisoner of war.
jĕnawi	long sword.

GLOSSARY

jĕnjulong	small-calibre guns.
jikalau	if.
jolong	project.
jumbul	(Dayak).

K.

kalok	curl; bend.
kampong	group of houses, hence village,
kambing	goat; *k. kachang,* part of *kĕris.*
kampilan	Ilanun sword.
kampoh	*tĕribok sa-k.* 2-edged str. dagger with hollow down centre.
kapak	axe.
kapitan	captain; *k. pĕrang,* army captain.
kata	speech.
katak	frog.
katok	shorts; kilt.
kĕban	matwork bag.
kĕchubong	helmet.
kĕlambu	bed-curtain; mosquito-net.
Kĕlantan	state in N.E. Mal. Penin.
kĕlewang	Indonesian sword.
kĕling	S. Indian.
kĕlok	wavy.
kĕmbar	making a pair.
kĕmboja	Cambodia.
kĕnchana	gold (poetically).
kĕnyang	repletion.
kĕpok	receptacle (for rice).
kĕraja'an	pertaining to a chief.
kĕrambit	claw dagger.
kĕrpai	powder horn.
Khĕrsani	fr. prov. of Khorasan, Persia.
kolak-kalek	shaking up and down.
kosong	empty; futile.
koteng	alone; *parang k.* chopper with hilt and blade in one piece.
kubit	a pinch.

kubu	stockade.
kuda	horse.
kudi	knife used in husbandry.
kuku	claw.
kulai	hanging; swaying.
kulit	skin; parchment.
kuning	yellow.
kujut	strangling.
kuran	sacred book of Islam.

L.

lada	pepper.
lading	cleaver.
lalang	grass (coarse).
lambai	brandish; *l. gajah,* part of *kĕris* blade.
lamina	scale mail armour.
langgai-tinggang	(Dayak).
lantak	ramming down.
lari	escape; flee.
latok	short; heavy.
lawi	curving feather, as cock's tail.
leher	neck.
lela	swivel gun.
lembing	spear with ridged blade.
lepa	tool.
lilin	wax.
lima	five.
limbang	depression.
lok	wave in *kĕris* blade.
lotong	variety of monkey.
luchun	gross insult.
lugu	content; self-satisfied.
lutang	knee.

M.

main	play.
Majapahit	Hindu-Jav. state: 1294-1400.
makan	to eat.

GLOSSARY

malu	ashamed.
mampai	false edge to a blade.
mata	eye.
mělawan	challenge; rivalry.
mělela	steel.
Měnangkabau	Malay territory in Sumatra.
měngerat	euphemism for death.
měnjadi	to become.
měriam	cannon.
měrubi	cf. *harubi*.
minum	to drink.
minyak	oil.
Muhammad	the Prophet; a proper name.
mulut	mouth.

P.

pagar	palisade.
pajab	children.
Pajajaram	Jav. kingdom, A.D. 1300-1500.
pakan	invulnerability.
pamor	damascened pattern on blade.
panah	bow; cf. *gandi*.
panchar	gushing forth.
pandai	expert.
pandak	short; cf. *pendek*.
panggalah	powder-horn.
panggong	platform; dam.
panjang	tall.
paring	cleaver; machete.
pari	skate; ray; sting ray.
parong	sinuous.
pasupati	Javanese *kěris*.
Patani	Malay dist. S. Siam.
pawang	magician; medicine man.
pědang	sword.
pěkakak	kingfisher.
pělantek	spring spear.
pěluru	cannon-ball; bullet.

pĕmanchong	finely cut; *pĕdang p.* execution sword.
pĕminggang	mid-ship.
pĕmuras	musketoon; blunderbuss.
pĕnampang	parapet of fort.
pĕndahan	javelin.
pendek	short.
pĕndok	metal casing, lower part of *kĕris* sheath.
pĕnggal	cut short; beheaded.
pĕnggalan	cf. *pĕnggal.*
pĕngatu	old type firearm.
pĕngawinan	balberdier; *tombak p.* spear of state.
pĕnimbul	*kĕbal p. 'subcutaneous* armour' of mercury.
pĕnunggal	to go off quickly; gallop.
pĕnyala	charm to secure invulnerability.
pĕnyalang	execution.
pĕnyakit	sickness.
pĕpatil	adze.
Perak	state on W. coast, Malay penin.
pĕrambut	invulnerability against weapons,
pĕranggi	iron-headed chopper.
pĕrbayangan	*kĕris* driven right thro' body.
pĕrdiul	*sĕnapang p.* muzzle loader.
pĕrempuan	woman.
pĕrisai	round shield.
pĕtĕrum	cartridge.
pichit	finger pressed.
pikam	point of arrow.
puchok	leaf-bud; point of growth.
pukul	strike; hit.
puloh	ten.
pun	suffix of emphasis; even, yet.
puru	*katak p.* toad.
puteh	white.
puting	head of blade; shank.

R.

radak	stabbing upwards.
raja	ruler.

GLOSSARY

rajawali	king of birds.
rajut	network; darning.
rambang	open.
rambu	fringe; tassel.
ranchang	pointing upwards.
ranggas	spiky mass of fallen timber.
rangin	long Indonesian shield.
rangking	large covered basket.
ranjau	caltrop.
rantai	chain.
rasul	apostle.
rĕbong	young bamboo shoot.
Rembau	dist. in Nĕgĕri Sembilan.
renchong	dagger (convex cutting edge).
rĕntaka	swivel gun.
rimbas	small adze or axe.
rotan	cane (for basketry).

S.

sa-bĕlah	one of a pair.
sabok	sash, of war-dress.
sagu-sagu	javelin.
sahaja	intentionally.
sakalian	all.
salang	execution with *kĕris*.
sampir	crosspiece of *kĕris* sheath.
sampul	caul.
sangga.	projecting guard or support.
sangsang	to hinder.
sepukal	straight *kĕris*.
sari	flower-like.
sarong	sheath; covering; skirt.
sayap	wing.
sĕladang	wild ox.
sĕlarak	closed; bolted.
sĕligi	wooden dart; javelin.
Sĕlinsing	dist. in Perak.
sĕloka	rhyme; jingle.

sĕmangat	indwelling spirit.
sĕmpana	sinuous.
sĕnapang	gun; musket; rifle.
sĕnjata	weapon.
sĕperti	like; similar to.
sĕrampang	trident.
sĕrai	palace.
sĕreng	sullen.
sĕri	honorific prefix.
sĕrunjong	sharpened stake used as spear.
sewar	dagger.
shamshir	sabre.
sigi	metal band on *kĕris* hilt or sheath.
sikap	mien; deportment.
sikapan	cf. *sikap*.
sikim	knife; sometimes sword.
silang	pointed end of *ganja*.
sodok	shovel.
sudu	spoon-shaped.
sumpah	oath.
sumpitan	blowpipe; *anak s.* blowpipe arrow.
sundang	sword *kĕris*.
Sulu	Borneo race.
sursur	outer walls.

T.

ta'	not; negative prefix.
tali	cord; belt.
tandang	travel; movement.
tangkai	stalk.
tambang	1. ferrying; 2. tying to post.
tameng	Indonesian round shield.
tapeh	long sarong or cover.
tarah	*t. baju*; Achehnese sword.
tĕbal	thick.
tĕgadas	obsolete cannon.
tekpi	trident.
tĕmbaga	brass.

tĕmbang	(Javanese) to sing.
tĕmin	metal band on dagger hilt cf. *sigi*.
tĕmpat	place.
tĕrajang	kicking down.
tĕrapang	casing of thin gold plate.
tĕrkepong	to besiege.
tĕrkul	rifle.
tĕrisula	trident.
tĕrus	straight.
tĕtĕrapan	cf. *tĕrapang*.
tilam upeh	Javanese *kĕris*.
tiga	three.
tikam	wounding by puncture.
tipu	trick.
tjoeriga	cf. *chĕriga* (Javanese).
tohok	stab downwards.
tombak	spear.
tomong	short, squat swivel gun.
torak	spindle shaped.
tayah	a thrusting pole.
Trĕngganu	state on E. coast of Malay penin.
tudong	shade for face: sun hat.
tujah	to stab down.
tujoh	seven.
tuju	sorcery by pointing.
tulale	(Javanese) cf. *Bĕlalai*.
tulang	bone.
tuli-tuli	loop of silver cord on *kĕris* sheath.
tulwar	Indian sword.
tumbok	to crush.
turtang	pledged.
tuwah	luck.

U.

ubat	drug.
ulu	cf. *hulu*.
umban	hurling from a sling.
undang	territorial chief.

utak	brain (also *otak*).
utar-utar	round shield hung with bells.

W.

wayang	stage play; cf. *kulit*.
wedung	Javanese weapon.

Y.

yang	who, which.

BIBLIOGRAPHY[1]

Beveridge, Henry; *A Comprehensive History of India*. London: Blackie & Son, 1867.

Gimlette, John D., M.R.C.S., L.R.C.P.; *Malay Poisons and Charm Cures*. J. & A. Churchill, 2nd edition, 1923.

Jasper, J. E.; *En Mas Pirngadie, De Inlandsche Kunstnijvereid In Nederlandsche Indie*. Mouton & Co., 1930.

Marsden, W., F.R.S.; *History of Sumatra*. Published by the Author, 1811.

Newbold, T. J.; *Political and Statistical Account of British Settlements in the Straits of Malacca*. 2 vols. John Murray, 1839.

Payne-Gallwey, Sir Ralph; *The Crossbow: Mediaeval and Modern, Military and Sporting: Its Construction History and Management, with a Treatise of the Balista and Catapult of the Ancients*. London: Longmans, Green, and Co., 1903.

Wilkinson, J. R., C.M.G.; *A Malay-English Dictionary*. 2nd edition, 1932.

Wright, Arnold & H. A. Cartwright, eds; *Twentieth Century Impressions of British Malaya: Its History, People, Commerce, Industries and Resources*. London: Lloyd's Greater Britain Pub. Co., 1908.

Raffles, Sir T. Stamford, F.R.S.; *History of Java*. Henry G. Bohn, 1844.

---

[1] To provide further clarification to Gardner's text, Beveridge, Payne-Gallwey and Wright & Cartwright have been added to the bibliography of the original edition. (Ed.)

ABOUT THE AUTHOR

Gerald Brousseau Gardner (1884-1964) was one of the more interesting products of the British colonial administration system in Southeast Asia. Born to a middle class family of Scottish descent, near Liverpool, England in 1884, he traced his ancestry to a woman burned as a witch in 1610—the relevance of this seemingly trivial piece of family arcanum to become clearer below. Gardner was initially a sickly child. His parents, believing that travel may help alleviate his asthmatic condition, left him in the care of his nurse, who first travelled Europe with the boy, then later, marrying an expatriate, relocated with the young Gardner to Ceylon. As a young man, Gardner worked on tea and rubber plantations in Ceylon and later in Borneo and Malaya.

Beginning in 1923 until his retirement in 1936, Gardner entered the employment of the British civil service in Southeast Asia as a customs official and inspector of rubber and opium production.

Gardner's time in the Far East facilitated his study of his twin fascinations of native spiritual beliefs and archaeology; it was during this period that he amassed a large collection of Malay weapons, including the *kĕris* (now more commonly *kris*) that led to his publication of the present, still authoritative although long out of print, volume. Of even more significance considering developments later in his later life, he nurtured a keen interest in and knowledge of Malay religion and magic.

Gardner returned to England with his wife on his retirement, and continued to pursue his archaeological interests. It was at this period of his life that he first reported experiencing psychic phenomena, and was also introduced to a group involved in the practice of contemporary witchcraft. He recorded that he was initiated into a British coven in 1939, when archaic laws still existed that banned the practice.

Gardner continued to learn and later to write about modern witchcraft, at first under an assumed name to avoid legal punishment, and later still openly, when British laws were revised in 1951 to decriminalize the practice. Believing himself to be an hereditary witch, Gardner formed his own coven the same year, going on to develop and record fresh versions of ritual and practice. His association with a fellow Englishman, Raymond Buckland, in 1963, led to the introduction of what is now know known as the 'Gardnerian Tradition' to America, thereafter to become the foundation of the modern practice of Wicca. His books on witchcraft remain seminal texts on the subject and he is remembered today among many practitioners as 'the father of the Wicca movement'.

Gardner died aboard ship, returning from travel to Lebanon, in 1964.

Gardner's publications included the following :
Keris and Other Malay Weapons, 1936
A Goddess Arrives, 1948
High Magic's Aid, 1949 (authored under the pseudonym 'Scire')
Witchcraft Today, 1954
The Story of the Famous Witches Museum at Castletown, Isle of Man, 1957
The Meaning of Witchcraft, 1959
Gardner's Book of Shadows (published posthumously, based on Gardner's unpublished mss. *Ye Booke of Ye Art Magical*)

Gardner's life and times have been the subject of at least three studies, as follows:
Bracelin, J. L.; *Gerald Gardner: Witch*, 1960
Heselton, Philip; *Wiccan Roots: Gerald Gardner and the Modern Witchcraft Revival*, 2000
——; *Gerald Gardner and the Cauldron of Inspiration*, 2003

www.ingramcontent.com/pod-product-compliance
Lightning Source LLC
Chambersburg PA
CBHW021846220426
43663CB00005B/420